CW00967630

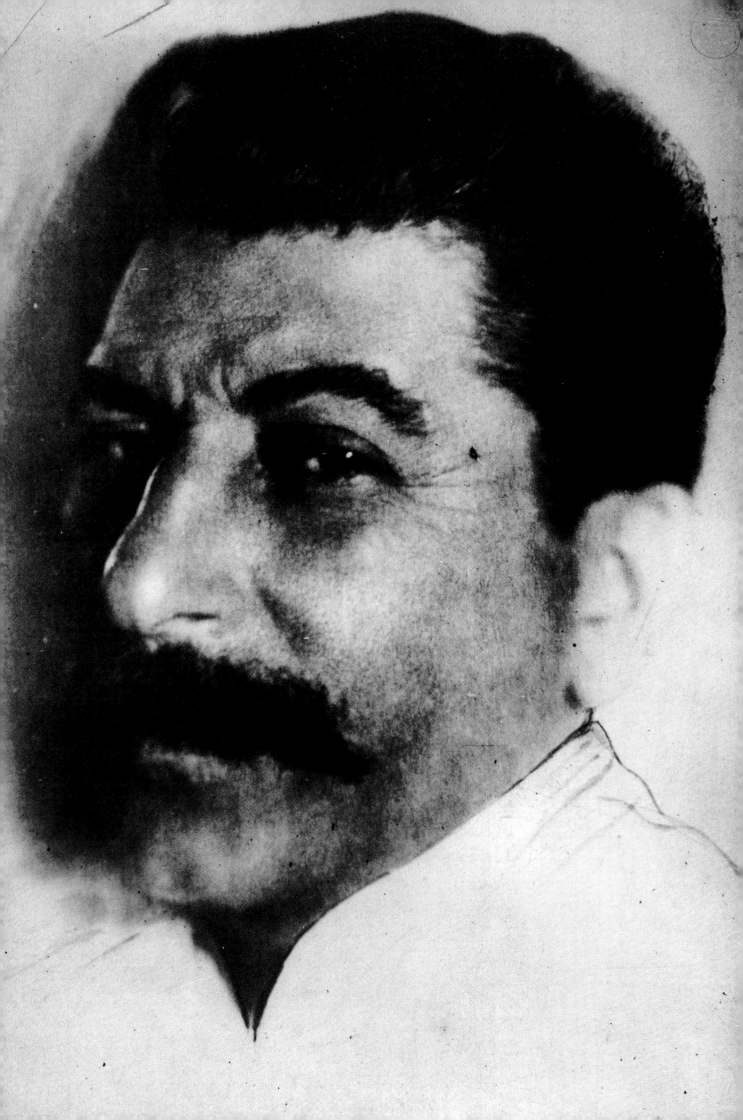

THE GREAT PURGES

Written by Isaac Deutscher
Edited by Tamara Deutscher
Designed by David King
Photographs from the David King Collection

Basil Blackwell
Oxford and New York

First published 1984
Copyright © David King and Tamara Deutscher 1984
Basil Blackwell Publisher, Oxford and New York

British Library Cataloguing in Publication Data
Deutscher, Isaac
The Great Purges
1. Political Purges — Soviet Union — History — Twentieth Century
2. Soviet Union — Politics and government — 1917-36
3. Soviet Union — Politics and government — 1936-53
I. Title II. King, David
947.084'2   DK267
ISBN 0-631-13923-0

Printed by Shadowdean Ltd., London

Preface

This book narrates — in authentic words and pictures — the horrifying story of what Trotsky called "the greatest forgery in the world's political history". Throughout the momentous decade of the 1930s the duel between Stalin and Trotsky occupied the centre of the Soviet political scene. Stalin harnessed the immense resources of power and propaganda of his state into the struggle against Trotskyism. He carried his anti-Trotsky campaign into every sphere of thought and activity both within the borders of the Soviet Union and outside it, among the communist confraternity abroad. The campaign reached its climax in 1936-38 when the world was treated to the macabre spectacle of the Moscow Trials, of which Stalin was the author, stage manager, producer, and prompter though he never appeared in court. The chief defendant, Trotsky, was 'tried' in absentia.

Deutscher explores the parallels and precedents of post-revolutionary purges in other epochs and other countries: after the European Protestant upheaval; in Cromwell's England; in the Great French Revolution. What made the Moscow spectacle so exceptionally hallucinatory in its sadism and masochism was the depth of self-humiliation into which the twentieth century tyrant hurled his broken adversaries denying them all possibility to defend their honour and die in dignity.

Nearly all the leaders of the October revolution, all members of Lenin's Politbureau, most commanders of the Red Army, many outstanding scientists and writers were denounced as terrorists, murderers, and wreckers, as foreign spies and traitors, and executed. The drama rose to its bizarre climax with Vyshinsky, the Prosecutor General, bellowing his fantastic indictment, and the defendants — all heroic revolutionaries — making their blood-chilling 'confessions' and declaring themselves guilty of monstrous crimes they could not have committed. "In presenting these scenes", said Deutscher, "I had to reconstruct a nightmare".

At the time of the Purges only one significant attempt to expose Stalin's frame-ups was made. This was the so-called Counter-trial under the chairmanship of John Dewey, held in Mexico City in 1937. The chief witness was Leon Trotsky who at the Moscow trials had been the chief defendant. The verdict of the Dewey Commission was an authoritative and unambiguous 'not guilty'. "Be it even over our bleaching bones, the truth will triumph" — thus Trotsky ended his refutation of Stalin's forgeries. Three years later, only a few streets away from the house where the Commission had held its sessions and these words were spoken, Stalin's agent drove an ice-pick into Trotsky's skull.

In Deutscher's historical documentary, the hangmen and the victims, Stalin and Vyshinsky on the one hand, and Lenin, Zinoviev, Kamenev, and Bukharin on the other, are the main actors. They as well as all the other dramatis personae speak with their authentic voices: all their utterances are taken from official records and public pronouncements, from archives and eye-witness accounts. The narrator intervenes only in order to make the context of the scenes and the background intelligible.

The authentic visual material which David King has been assembling for many years, adds another dimension to the written text and effectively illustrates the haunting quality of the historic drama.

Tamara Deutscher, May 1984

The text was originally written for the Home Service of the BBC, at the initiative of the late Lawrence Gilliam, head of Features Department, and transmitted twice in the course of 1965. It was also transmitted in Germany, Sweden and the USA.

"He Will Slay Us..."

'All arts have produced their marvels; only the art of government had produced nothing but monstrosities' – so said a great French revolutionary. The most shocking of all the monstrosities of Stalin's government were the Great Purges, when an immense wave of terror swept the U.S.S.R., and they culminated in the Moscow trials of 1936–8. Decades have passed since then. Yet the world has not forgotten the purges, which are the heaviest single burden on the communist conscience. Their horror still haunts us: Mao and Khrushchev have argued about Stalin's role in those purges – and, incidentally, about Khrushchev's also.

Khrushchev: Comrades, Stalin employed mass terror when there was no need for it. Thousands upon thousands of honest and innocent communists died as a result of monstrous falsifications . . . They were forced to bring false charges against both themselves and others. These slanderous confessions were extorted from them. The N.K.V.D. prepared lists of persons to be tried by the military tribunal . . . The sentences were ready in advance. Comrades, these mass arrests did tremendous harm to our country, and to the cause of socialist progress.

Mao Tse-tung and his followers were trying to defend Stalin's record, yet even they were puzzled and baffled by the Great Purges. Peking commented: 'How are we to assess Stalin's role in these events? This is a grave, difficult and complicated question – a question of world-wide importance. But a final answer to it can hardly be reached in the present century.'

What then were the Great Purges?

What was their cause? Who were their victims? What were the consequences? And were the purges a purely Russian or Soviet phenomenon? There are some parallels in the histories of other countries. Quite apart from the terror of the Holy Inquisition, which was different in character, each of the great revolutions of modern times – the European Protestant upheaval, the English Puritan revolution and the great French revolution – had its own version of the purges.

In Germany the Reformation, being both a religious and a social upheaval, opened an epoch of bourgeois revolution and peasant war. As he formed his party, Luther at first included in it the most radical and heretical elements. As Friedrich Engels put it:

Engels: When in 1517 the opposition against the dogma and the organization of the Catholic Church was first raised by Luther, it still had no definite character . . . it did not exclude any trend of opinion which went further. It could not do so because the first moment of the struggle demanded that all opposing elements be united, the most aggressive revolutionary energy be utilized, and the totality of the existing heresies fighting the Catholic orthodoxy be represented . . . Luther's sturdy peasant nature asserted itself in the stormiest fashion in the first period of his activities.

Luther: If the raging madness (of the Roman churchmen) were to continue, it seems to me no better counsel and remedy could be found against it than that kings and princes sally forth, arm themselves, attack those evil people who have poisoned the entire world and once and for all make an end to this game, *with arms not with words* . . . Why do we

not seize, with arms in hand, all those evil teachers of perdition, those Popes, Bishops, Cardinals and the entire crew of Roman Sodom? Why do we not wash our hands in their blood?

Luther's call raised men of all classes to their feet, the bourgeoisie, the lower nobility, the craftsmen, the peasants and even the princes. With this multiplicity of social forces arrayed behind it, the camp of the Reformation was inevitably divided. With his translation of the Bible, Luther put a weapon in the hands of the revolutionary heretics among the peasants and the plebeian masses – the Anabaptists and the other sects, who found their leaders in Thomas Münzer, Nikolas Storch, Ulrich Schmid and other preachers of the Millennium. Even before Luther, Münzer, who established himself as a preacher at Alstedt in Thuringia, eliminated Latin from his church services and introduced other reforms which anticipated the most extreme forms of Protestantism. As this revolution was taking place in religious forms, the theological argument dominated all its debates. Engels says of Münzer:

Engels: Under the cloak of Christian forms, he preached a kind of pantheism, which curiously resembles the modern speculative mode of contemplation, and at times even approached atheism.

The insurgent peasants formulated their requests in the famous Twelve Articles in which they demanded an elective priesthood and abolition of tithes, the abolition of serfdom and similar radical desiderata. Nearly four centuries before the Russian revolution the participants

Right: Stalin and Khrushchev.
Opposite page:
Martin Luther by Lucas Cranach

TOMAS MVNCER PREDIGER ZV ALSTET IN DVRINGE

in the German peasant war already raised the red flag over their camps, the flag that Germany once gave the world. It goes without saying that the Lutheran princes, nobility and bourgeoisie were terrified by the peasant revolt in the country and the rising of all plebeian elements in the towns. Luther himself, after a period of hesitation, turned against the peasants, against Münzer and other radical heretics. The Reformation had to be purged of its extreme elements, just as some of the modern revolutions were to be purged later. And the bitter invective and the violent language of the purges presently resounded in the Lutheran camp. This is how Luther called all his adherents to struggle 'against the murderers and plundering hordes of the peasants'.

Luther: They should be broken to pieces, strangled and stabbed, secretly and openly by everybody who can do it, and be mindful that there cannot be anything more poisonous, more harmful, more devilish than a rebellious person who has to be killed just as one must kill a mad dog . . . strike, strangle . . . here whoever may be able to . . .

This call, 'Shoot the mad dogs!', will be heard in centuries to come in English, French and Russian, in all the great purges. It sums up the emotional intensity, the fanaticism and the fury with which Luther, Cromwell, Robespierre and Stalin, each in his own way, were suppressing the opponents in their own camp. This is Luther again, speaking in May 1529 about the insurgent peasants:

Luther: We must pray for them that they obey. Where they do not there should not be much mercy. Let the guns roar among them, or else they will make it a thousand times worse.

And the guns roared. There is no need to recount here the vicissitudes of the peasant war, which are well known. The stakes were high, although Münzer's revolutionary party formed a small minority even among the great mass of the rebellious peasants. Marx and Engels spoke of Münzer's 'brilliant anticipation' of modern communism.

Engels: By the kingdom of God (which he preached) Münzer understood nothing other than a state of society without class differences, without private property, without any more state powers opposed to the members of society. All existing authorities, as far as they did not submit and join the revolution, must be overthrown, all work and all property must be shared in common, and complete equality must be introduced. A union of the people was to be organized to realize this programme, not only throughout Germany, but throughout the entire Christian world . . .

Unlike the purges in the French and the Russian revolutions, the purges of the Reformation, similar in this respect to the purges of the Puritan English revolution, took the form not of court trials, but of pitched battles. The peasant rebellions were drowned in blood all over Western and South-Western Germany. Of the 8,000 peasants alone who were with Münzer in his last battle at Schlachtberg 5,000 were slaughtered.

Engels: Münzer, wounded in the head, was discovered in a house and captured . . . He was put on the rack in the presence of the princes, and then decapitated. He went to his death with the same courage with which he had lived. He was at the most twenty-eight when he was executed. Pfeifer was also executed and besides him a great number of others.

Historians may argue to what an extent these purges can really be considered as precedents to the purges in modern revolutions. If we describe as purges the bloody inner struggle within the party of the revolution, can Luther and Münzer be said to have belonged to the same party? Engels, for instance, treats them as representatives of two different parties, each leading different social forces. He speaks of Luther's party as the party of reform and treats only Münzer as the head and the ideologue of the party of a premature and doomed revolution. But the fact remains that at the beginning of the Reformation all these forces stood together, if only for a short time, and Luther and Münzer took the same direction, even if Münzer was at times ahead of Luther. It may also be argued that, just as the purges in the French and the Russian revolutions caused confusion, demoralization and a decline of moral energy in the

party of the revolution, so the peasant war and the Lutheran heresy-hunt brought about an inner paralysis and a stagnation in the Reformation. And it was to take about three centuries before German radical historians began to rehabilitate Thomas Münzer and the other victims of the purges of the German Reformation. It seems that a closer parallel to the modern purges may be found in the English Puritan revolution, although the only event which the textbooks describe as a purge is the famous Colonel Pride's purge. It occurred in 1648, shortly before the trial and execution of Charles I. The King's enemies were clamouring for the overthrow of the monarch; but in the House of Commons the Presbyterians, the moderates of the Puritan revolution, still commanded a majority; and they were anxious to save Charles. Cromwell had to break or disperse the Presbyterian majority before he could destroy the King and proclaim the Commonwealth. On 6 December 1648, Colonel Pride, one of Cromwell's soldiers, stood at the door of the House of Commons and prevented 140 M.P.s from entering the House – his soldiers dragged many of them away into custody. Cromwell and Fairfax behaved as if they had nothing to do with that act of violence; but Colonel Pride paved the way for Cromwell's ascendancy.

Pride's Purge is not really comparable with any of the Great Purges, in the sense that the term has now acquired, although it was a crucial act of violence. The Great Purges occur at a different phase of the revolution and in a special context. Each of the great modern revolutions, the Puritan, the Jacobin and the Bolshevik, began against the background of the multi-party system, or at least of an open contest between the various political parties. As the events unfolded, the extreme party, the party of the revolution, destroyed all other parties, conservatives and moderates alike, and established its own exclusive rule, or, as we say now, the single-party system. Cromwell, Robespierre and Lenin did this. No sooner, however, is the single-party system established than a new struggle begins within the single party – and it is to this phase that the Great Purges belong. At the root of the new struggle lies the insecurity of the revolutionary party – its fear of counter-revolutionary contradiction, controversy and opposition. Having crushed all other parties, the new rulers find that they have not yet eliminated contradiction and opposition. Among their own followers, various factions make their appearance and are soon at loggerheads with each other. One faction holds that the revolution has gone too far; another that it has not gone far enough. Some, weary of the continuous upheaval, are anxious to bring revolutionary violence to a halt; others, disillusioned with the meagre results of the upheaval, wish it to go on. The single party is in danger of splitting into several parties; and to forestall this, its leader seeks to reduce its various factions to silence.

The Great Purges, therefore, are not incidents in the struggle between the party of the revolution and its conservative and moderate enemies. The Great

**Above: Oliver Cromwell.
Top left: methods of punishment during the Peasant Wars**

Purges affect the revolutionary party itself, and result from its internal struggles. They lead to the suppression, or rather the self-suppression, of the revolutionary party; they replace the rule of the single party with the rule of a single leader.

A closer parallel to the Great Purges is found in Cromwell's suppression of the radical agitators in his Model Army, of the Levellers, the True Levellers, the Diggers, the Fifth Monarchy Men and their like. These groups and sects were of the flesh and blood of Puritanism. They had been Cromwell's most energetic and devoted followers. They had formed the left wing of the revolutionary party. They were the Puritan radicals and ultra-radicals. Over three centuries ago, they fought for a general and equal franchise; some of them already dreamed of a society of equals. No wonder they were disenchanted with Cromwell's Commonwealth, especially when they saw Cromwell spring to the defence of property and of privilege, establishing his own personal rule and becoming England's uncrowned monarch. At once they turned against him and vehemently denounced him. 'Is this what we have fought for?' – the cry occurs after every revolution. Barely a month after the execution of Charles I, John Lilburne came forward with his pamphlet, *England's New Chains Discovered: An Impeachment of High Treason Against Oliver Cromwell*. The radical agitators in the Model Army, the Levellers and the True Levellers echoed Lilburne's denunciation: 'The poorest he that is in England hath a life to live as the greatest he . . . Unless we that are poor have some part of the land to live upon freely as well as the gentry, it cannot be a free commonwealth . . . We are English soldiers engaged for the freedom of England and not outlandish mercenaries to butcher these people, to serve the pernicious ends of ambition and will or any person under Heaven.'

In the Council of State, Cromwell pounded the table with his fist, and thus addressed Bradshaw (Chairman of the Council and Milton's brother-in-law):

Cromwell: I tell you, Sir, there is no other way to deal with these men, the Agitators, but to break them into pieces.

John Lilburne spent the rest of his life in the Tower of London, in exile in Holland, on the island of Jersey and, finally, within the walls of Dover Castle.

Other rebels were imprisoned, exiled or executed.

Yet in one essential respect these Cromwellian purges differed from those of the Jacobins and Bolsheviks. The Puritan Revolution, for all its flaming religious passion, was military in character and methods. Its main agent was the army, not some civilian political party. Consequently, the Cromwellian purges took the form of pitched battles rather than of monster trials. The Levellers and radical agitators exercised considerable influence upon large sections of the New Model Army. Entire regiments rose in arms against Cromwell, marched from Salisbury to Abingdon, captured Northampton and stirred up various other counties. Cromwell and Fairfax suppressed these revolts by force of arms. Some of the defeated Levellers recanted and then served Cromwell.

On 7 June 1649, Cromwell and Fairfax celebrated their triumph over the Levellers. At a splendid banquet at the Grocer's Hall, the City of London hailed them as the saviours of property. Yet the ideas of the Levellers continued to haunt England; and five years after that celebration, when opening the first Parliament of the Protectorate, Cromwell thus inveighed against those in England who were longing for the abolition of class distinctions:

Cromwell: A noble man, a gentleman, a yeoman, 'the distinction of these': that is a good interest of the Nation, and a great one! The 'natural' Magistracy of the Nation was it not almost trampled under foot, under despite and contempt, by men of Levelling principles? I beseech you, for the orders of men and ranks of men, did not that Levelling principle tend to the reducing of all to an equality? Did it 'consciously' think to do so; or did it 'only unconsciously' practise towards that for property and interest? At all events, what was the purport of it but to make the Tenant as liberal a fortune as the Landlord? And that the thing did 'and might well' extend far, is manifest; because it was a pleasing voice to all Poor Men, and truly not unwelcome to all Bad Men.

A few months later, at the dissolution of Parliament, Cromwell once again vented his fear and detestation of these premature egalitarians.

Cromwell: It is some satisfaction if a Commonwealth must perish, that it perish by men and not by the hands of persons differing little from beasts! That if it must needs suffer, it should rather suffer from rich men than from poor men, who, as Solomon says, 'when they oppress leave nothing behind them, but are a sweeping rain'.

Nevertheless, purges did not loom in the English revolution as large as they did in the French and the Russian. The Levellers had few, if any, eminent political leaders; they were the rank and file of the revolutionary party. It was therefore relatively easy for Cromwell to suppress them. Robespierre and Stalin had a far more difficult job – each of them had to contend with far more dangerous and influential opponents. The Levellers who rose against Cromwell were ensigns, corporals, privates. Carlyle, who as a historian sides with Cromwell, had this to say of them:

Carlyle: To die the Leveller Corporals; strong they after their sort, for the Liberties of England; resolute to the very death. Misguided Corporals! But history will not refuse these poor Corporals her tributary sigh.

History indeed has not refused her tributary sigh to these victims of Cromwell's purges. Generations of British socialists and democrats have honoured them as the fore-runners and martyrs of modern democracy and socialism.

Let us now turn to the *épurations* of the great French revolution. The scene is Paris; the time, early spring 1794. Louis XVI and Marie Antoinette have been executed. France is an embattled Republic, in the throes of the civil war, struggling against British, Prussian and Austrian intervention. The Jacobin Party, led by Robespierre, Danton and Saint-Just, dominates the Revolutionary Convention. This is the moment of the Jacobins' supreme triumph. They have crushed all the parties that were opposed to the proclamation of the Republic. But they have already lost Marat, their chief leader, who was assassinated by Charlotte Corday; and at the very moment of their triumph they fall out among themselves. Three factions are then formed within the Jacobin party: the Dantonists, followers of Danton, stand on the right; Robespierre and Saint-Just lead the men of the middle, the Centre faction; while to the left there are the Hébertists, followers of Hébert, the radicals and ultra-radicals, the *enragés* and the men of the Commune of Paris.

Danton and his friends are already worried by the excesses of revolution; they seek to reassure the new bourgeoisie and to end or mitigate the reign of terror. Robespierre's men, backed by the Hébertists and the Commune of Paris, do not think that the time has come to call a halt to revolution and terror – they would rather press ahead with both. For a time Danton and his friends try to keep in step with the rest of the party; but before the end of the year 1793, Danton begins to attack the Hébertists, who are reputed to be atheists. This is how Danton spoke at the Convention:

Danton: Let us have no prepossessions. If we do not honour the priest of error and the priest of fanaticism neither let us honour the priest of disbelief. We wish to serve the people. I demand that anti-religious masquerades in the Convention shall cease.

On the same day, Danton spoke about one of the anti-Republican plots, a real or imaginary plot said to be directed from England and inspired or financed by Pitt's government. The Convention had before it at this moment a motion calling for death sentences on the conspirators. Danton supported the motion but very ambiguously.

Danton: The Committee should prepare a report about *what is called* this foreign-inspired conspiracy. Our people clamoured for a Terror, and our people were right. But the people want this Terror to fulfil its real purpose, they want it directed against the aristocrats, the egoists, the conspirators and traitors. The time has not yet come to show clemency. This is still a time for national inflexibility and vengeance.

At this point the Hébertists and other Left Jacobins already charge Danton with lukewarmness, and indulgence to the enemies of the Republic.

Danton: I wish to justify myself in the eyes of the people, who should not find it hard to recognize my innocence and my love of liberty. Have I really changed so much? Has my face, the face of a free man, suddenly changed its appearance? Am I no longer he whom our enemies have persecuted above all others?

'The Death of Marat' by Jacques-Louis David.

'Marat at the Moment of Death' by David. 'Unable to corrupt me, they have killed me'

On 2 February 1794, the Convention sat in judgement upon two men, Vincent and Ronsin, both Hébertists and both Danton's opponents. Danton, frightened by the havoc already wrought by the Reign of Terror among the revolutionists themselves, came out to defend Vincent and Ronsin.

Danton: It should be an unshakeable principle that veterans of the revolution, who have rendered constant and well-known services to Liberty, must never be treated as suspects. I know that the violent and impetuous characters of Vincent and Ronsin may have led them to act wrongly towards this or that individual. But just as I am ready to accuse my best friend if my conscience tells me that he is guilty, so today I wish to defend Ronsin and Vincent.

However, Danton did not manage to persuade the Jacobins that the veterans of the revolution should be above suspicion. Robespierre, Saint-Just and Couton suspected the Left Jacobins and felt themselves threatened by the Levellers of the Commune of Paris. They were determined to destroy them. Danton, likewise, was afraid of the egalitarians of the Left and even more afraid of breaking with Robespierre. And so, despite his forebodings, he decided to support the purge of the Left Jacobins. On 13 March 1794, at a session of the Comité de Salut Public, Saint-Just indicts the leaders of the Left: Hébert, famous as Père Duchesne, Anacharsis Cloots, the 'Orator of the Human Race', as he was called, Ronsin and others. Saint-Just denounces them, not as radicals or ultra-radicals, who by their excesses might have harmed their own cause, but as enemies of the people, as Royalist plotters, as English agents and spies.

Saint-Just: We have discovered a conspiracy, here, within our Republic, a plot hatched abroad. Its purpose has been to corrupt the Republic and so to prevent its consolidation; to prepare starvation for the people; and to forge new chains for Liberty. All vices have leagued and armed themselves against our Republic. Monsieur Pitt, the British Prime Minister, is of course the chief author of this conspiracy.

Here is one of the keynotes of all great purges. The men in the dock are presented as agents of the old regime; as saboteurs, wreckers and foreign spies. In order to make such charges reasonably credible, a few genuine Royalists, an obscure spy or a few ordinary criminals and felons are put in the dock alongside the chief defendants. The French used to call this technique *l'amalgame*. There was a hint of this even in Cromwell's purges, for Cromwell also indicted the Levellers as the agents of England's foreign enemies. But in the Cromwellian purges, such accusations were still incidental; whereas in the Jacobin purges (and then in the Bolshevik) they occupied a central place. Paris was stunned. Who could believe that the famous Père Duchesne and the Orator of the Human Race were spies and enemies of the Republic? Only quite recently everyone had witnessed the Republican ardour and revolutionary deeds of these accused leaders. Saint-Just needed all his great ingenuity and eloquence to make his charges carry conviction. He argued that Hébert and his friends had merely postured as good Jacobins, but had in fact dissembled their real purpose. They had worn revolutionary masks all the time, said Saint-Just, for otherwise they would not have been in a position to act.

Saint-Just: If anyone nowadays were to run through the streets of Paris shouting 'Give us a King', he would be arrested and would perish on the spot. A Royalist nowadays must be a dis-sembler. We must not judge people by their speeches and appearances. There is in our very midst a party which is opposed to Liberty, a *party of dissemblers.*

Note how Saint-Just is here using an element of truth to support a falsehood. Obviously, a true Royalist living in Paris in the fifth year of the revolution had to conceal his views and activities. That was common knowledge. But how could one know who did and who did not conceal his views? Anyone might be a dissembler, even someone known as a veteran of the revolution. And conversely, any veteran of the revolution, any influential, meritorious and famous leader of the revolutionary party could be denounced as a dissembler; and destroyed.

In this way Saint-Just and Robespierre confused public opinion and fanned a suspicion so intense and morbid that, no longer able to tell friend from foe, people accepted even the most fantastic accusations. Who knows, many a Jacobin murmured, perhaps our supposed leaders have in fact been our enemies and have succeeded in lulling our vigilance? This collapse of all trust and confidence accompanied the purges, and, like a moral earthquake, it removed the ground from under the Jacobin party. On 24 March 1794 Hébert, Cloots, Ronsin and their friends were guillotined.

Robespierre's death mask.
Opposite page:
contemporary print of the guillotine

Paris lived in a fever. The reign of terror reached a pitch of insanity. Day in, day out, the Comité de Salut Public compiled lists of suspects. Day in, day out, crowds watched the tumbrils filled with Jacobins as they rolled on their way to the guillotine in the Place de la Révolution or elsewhere.

No sooner had Robespierre destroyed the Jacobin Left than he felt his own position insecure – because the Jacobin Right, the Dantonists, had been strengthened by the defeat of the Left. And so, on 31 March 1794, only a week after the execution of the Hébertists, Robespierre was already indicting Danton, Camille Desmoulins, Fabre d'Eglantine and their friends.

Robespierre: *Danton, tu as servi la tyrannie!* Danton, you have supported tyranny! Dare you deny it? You have sold yourself to the wicked conspirators against Liberty. Danton, you have worked to corrupt public morals! You have wished to stage an insurrection in Paris! You have sought to conciliate the enemies of the Republic. You have never felt any enmity towards them, Danton. You have been General Dumouriez' accomplice, and the accomplice of the Duke of Orléans. It is even said that you had secret conferences with Marie Antoinette at the Temple. And you, Camille Desmoulins, you were first Danton's dupe and then his accomplice. You have been Danton's catspaw.

Danton and his friends were already imprisoned. It was in their absence that Saint-Just reported on their case to the Convention, addressing himself personally to the absent Danton. He sounded exactly like an echo of Robespierre.

Saint-Just: *Danton, tu as servi la tyrannie! Mauvais citoyen, tu as conspiré!* Danton, you have supported tyranny! Oh, evil citizen, you have been conspiring! Malignant man, you have compared to a harlot the voice of public opinion. You have said that honour is ridiculous, and that glory and posterity are follies. Thus you have curried favour with the aristocracy. For six months, Danton and his friends were hatching their plot at the very heart of the government. Then hosts of enemies were attacking us from all sides. The moment was well chosen; Alsace was newly invaded. The Spaniards and English had seized Toulon. Perpignan was threatened. Our unfortunate armies fought in the North, at Mont Blanc, in the

Vendée; everywhere. It was then that Hébert's faction clamoured for a constitution; for they sought to provoke a chaos full of danger and adversity, and to replace our revolutionary government with some other and feeble regime. Danton also called for a constitution. And remember that at this time Danton often dined with the English at the rue Grande-Batelière.

Thus the leaders of the revolutionary party were again branded as foreign agents and spies. Any less grotesque accusation would not have been enough to incite the population of Paris or persuade them that these men deserved to be guillotined. However, by levelling such charges against their erstwhile comrades, Robespierre and Saint-Just were themselves reducing the revolutionary regime to an absurdity and were destroying popular confidence. Unwittingly Saint-Just himself parodied the reasoning behind the great purges:

Saint-Just: The popular revolution was the mere surface of a volcano of foreign plots. Those who have conspired under the veil of patriotism, say now that, like Saturn, the revolution is devouring all

Opposite page: Robespierre reduced to executing the executioner because everyone else in France had been guillotined. Caricature by Hercy

her children. Hébert said this at his trial; and now all those who see themselves exposed, and who tremble, repeat it once more. Not so: the revolution does not devour her children, she devours her enemies.

The trial of Danton and his friends was a farce. The verdicts were ready beforehand. The President of the Tribunal constantly interrupted Danton, and used the crudest tricks to silence him. But Danton roared from the dock. Outside the court there waited a huge tense crowd; and as Danton's thunderous voice reverberated across the Seine, the multitude loudly expressed sympathy with him. This is how Danton spoke – interrupted by the President, but defying his accusers:

Danton: My voice, which has so often been heard defending the cause of the people, my voice will find it easy to repudiate calumny. The cowards who slander me, dare they come here and attack me to my face? Let them show themselves, and I shall cover them with ignominy. I have said this once, and I will say it again: *Mon domicile est bientôt dans le néant, mon nom au Panthéon.* My home will soon be in the void, but my name will be in the Pantheon.

President of the Court: Danton, your heated tone is unsuited to this court – refrain from such displays of false audacity.

Danton: False audacity? No doubt individual audacity may be reprehensible. But audacity in a national cause, this kind of audacity is permissible – and even necessary in a revolution; of this kind of audacity I am proud. When I see myself so grievously, so unjustly accused, how shall I contain the indignation that rises in me? Can one, should one, expect a cool answer from a revolutionary like myself? I am charged with having sold myself. But men of my kind have no market price. Such men have the stamp of liberty, and of the republican genius, indelibly printed on their brows. And you, Saint-Just, you will answer to posterity for this calumny. You say I aimed at restoring the monarchy . . . Oh, yes, I can tell you in some detail how I did that, how I provoked the restoration of royalty and even how I protected the royal tyrant. Only one thing is very strange in all this: how is it that the National Convention has been so blind as to see nothing of all this until today? What miracle has so suddenly opened its eyes to my true role?

President of the Court: (REPEATEDLY RINGS THE BELL AND SHOUTS): Danton, can you not hear my bell?

Danton: *Monsieur le Président*, the voice of a man who defends his life will not be drowned by the sound of your bell.

With such magnificent intrepidity, Danton defended himself to the end. Back in his cell he said to his co-prisoners:

Danton: They think they can do without me. They are mistaken. I was Europe's statesman. They know what void will remain when my head has fallen. As for myself, I can only laugh. I have enjoyed the brief moment of my existence. I have caused enough commotion on this earth.

CY·GYT
TOUTE
LA FRANCE

21

'Act of Justice', an allegory on the Terror inspired by the death of Robespierre. His is the head wearing spectacles and crowned by daggers

I have savoured life. Now it is time to sleep.

Lamartine thus describes the scene of Danton's execution:

Lamartine: Danton was the last to mount the scaffold. Never had he mounted a rostrum more superbly and impressively. He placed himself squarely on the scaffold. He seemed to take the measure of it, as if it were his pedestal. He eyed – almost with pity – those who stood to the right and left of him. Look at me well, his posture seemed to tell them – for you will never see my like. For a moment, a natural emotion dissolved his pride. He remembered his young wife, his eyes moistened, and he cried out: Oh, my beloved, I shall see you no more! Then, as if reproaching himself, he said loudly: *Allons, Danton, point de faiblesse.* Come now, Danton, no weakness. Turning to the executioner, he said in a commanding voice:

Danton: You will show my head to the people, will you not? It is well worth showing.

Lamartine: His head fell. The executioner lifted it, put it into a basket and walked with it around the scaffold. The crowd applauded.

With the destruction of both the Left and the Right factions, the Hébertists and the Dantonists, the Jacobin party was reduced to a rump. Robespierre, Saint-Just and Couton exercised full power and hoped to consolidate it. Yet Paris was full of their enemies, full of the wreckage of the old aristocracy, the hidden Legitimistic royalists, and the followers of the Duke of Orléans; and there were the cowed and silent friends of the Girondists and of the Dantonists and Hébertists . . . the social turmoil was unabated. The upstarts and the *nouveaux riches* of Paris were impatient with the austerities of Robespierre's rule; and the poor were weary of starvation and terror.

Robespierre's government was left at the heart of a void; and a plot, the plot of the so-called Thermidorians, was being hatched in the Convention. On 9th Thermidor, according to the revolutionary calendar, that is on 27 July 1794, less than four months after Danton's execution, Robespierre and his government were overthrown. They faced the same accusations with which they had overwhelmed the Hébertists

and the Dantonists; and they were given not the slightest chance to defend themselves. Saint-Just stood at the rostrum of the Convention for four hours, with the manuscript of his last speech in his hands – the uproar from the floor did not allow him to speak. Silent, erect and courageous he gazed haughtily at his enemies. On the next day he made his last journey, the journey to the guillotine. By Saint-Just's side in the tumbril lay Robespierre, his jaw broken, his head covered with blood. Among the last words penned by Saint-Just are these:

Saint-Just: What have we made of human reason? It would be better to flee into a desert, to find independence there, or to make friends of the wild beasts. It is better to forsake a world in which no strength is left either in crime or in virtue, in which nothing remains but dismay and contempt.

Thus fell the Jacobin party; and its overthrow paved the way for the Directory, the Consulate and the empire of Napoleon Bonaparte.

Another hundred and ten years passed; Brussels and London witnessed an important preliminary to the Russian revolution of the twentieth century. In these two capital cities, a Congress of the small and clandestine Russian Social Democratic Party assembled in July 1903. At the Congress a split occurred between two factions, the Bolsheviks and the Mensheviks. That party had been born which was destined to carry out the October revolution of 1917. Its leader was Lenin. Not many of the participants of the Congress were aware of the momentous significance of the event. But a few were; and in their thoughts, memories of the great French revolution were mingled with foreboding. George Plekhanov, founder of Russian Marxism, philosopher, critic and political leader, was the most celebrated personality at the Congress. Lenin modestly considered himself to be his disciple. At the moment of the schism, Plekhanov uneasily supported Lenin. But, watching Lenin and listening to his speeches, he remarked wistfully:

Plekhanov: It is of such stuff that the Robespierres of the world are made.

One of the youngest yet most prominent actors at the Congress was twenty-three-

George Plekhanov

year-old Leon Trotsky. He joined the Mensheviks and vehemently inveighed against Lenin.

Trotsky: Like a new Robespierre, Lenin is trying to transform the modest Council of our party into an omnipotent Committee of Public Safety. Comrades, I do not really intend to compare Lenin with Robespierre. The leader of the Bolsheviks is a mere parody of Robespierre, whom he resembles no more than vulgar farce may resemble great historic tragedy. If we were to adopt Lenin's ideas about our party, the result would be that the party organization, the caucus, would substitute itself for the organization; until finally, a single dictator substituted himself for the Central Committee.

Lenin was not at all embarrassed by these comparisons and accusations. He replied:

Lenin: A revolutionary social democrat *is*, and must be, a Jacobin; but one who is inseparably linked with the organization of the working class, and who is conscious of its class interests.

Against this, Trotsky argued that a Marxist, that is a social democrat or communist, cannot be and must not be a Jacobin.

Trotsky: Robespierre and his friends had their own metaphysical idea of truth, their *Vérité*; but they did not believe that their *Vérité* could win the hearts and minds of the people. They looked around them with morbid suspicion; they saw enemies creeping out of every cranny. Therefore, the Jacobins drew a sharp distinction between themselves and the rest of the world. They drew it with the blade of the guillotine. They spared no human hecatombs to build the pedestal for their Truth. The counterpart of their absolute faith in a metaphysical idea was their absolute distrust of living people. Comrades, the social democrat and the Jacobin stand for different and even opposite worlds, doctrines, tactics, mentalities. The Jacobins were utopian dreamers; we aspire to express the true, the objective, trend of history. They were idealists; we are materialists. They were rationalists; we are dialecticians. They chopped off heads; we seek to enlighten them. A Jacobin tribunal would have tried the whole international labour movement on the charge of moderation. Marx's lion head would have been the first to roll beneath the guillotine. Maximilien Robespierre used to say: I know only two parties, the good and the evil citizens. This aphorism is engraved on the heart of Maximilien Lenin. Lenin's malicious and morally repulsive suspicion is a downright caricature of the tragic Jacobin intolerance.

Yet fourteen years later, in 1917, Trotsky joined hands with Lenin, and together they led the Bolshevik Party in the October revolution. But soon thereafter the party was deeply divided. This was late in the First World War, in which Tsarist Russia had been Britain's and France's ally. Should Bolshevik Russia go on fighting, or should she contract out of the war and sign a separate peace with Germany? That was the question. There was a peace faction and a war faction – the former headed by Lenin, the latter by Bukharin. Trotsky stood between the two factions and coined the famous phrase: Neither war nor peace!

So vehement grew the inner-party struggle that all Bolshevik leaders became deeply apprehensive. They began to wonder whether some inexorable logic of revolution was not already driving them along the road the Jacobins had travelled, the road at the end of which were the Great Purges and the Thermidorian coup d'état. Early in 1918, at a meeting of the Politbureau, there occurred this hitherto unrecorded episode: Bukharin had come to the meeting with what he called the *Draft of an Anti-Thermidorian Catechism*. This consisted of rules and regulations designed to restrain inner party controversy and to prevent it from degenerating into a fratricidal struggle. Bukharin proposed that his *Anti-Thermidorian Catechism* should be widely circulated among party members. All those present at the meeting read the document and waited for Lenin to express his opinion. After a moment of reflection Lenin spoke:

Lenin: Comrades, I see no need to circulate this among party members. I do not see what purpose any such catechism may serve. I trust we shall never seek to settle our inner-party differences in a Jacobin manner. But if events were ever to drive us that way, if any of us were ever to be tempted to settle our differences by means of the guillotine, then God have mercy on us, for no anti-Thermidorian catechism will help us then. It is a childish idea, Nikolai Ivanovich, that we could stop or forestall so fatal a development with the help of a sheet of paper like this.

The incident reveals how very early – and with what inward shudders – the Bolshevik leaders were thinking it possible that the Russian revolution might fall into the pattern of the Great Purge. True, Bukharin's *Anti-Thermidorian Catechism* never saw the light – and there was as yet no need for it.

Left: an early Bolshevik committee, with Trotsky seated second from left and Zinoviev seated second from right. Opposite page: Nikolai Bukharin.

Overleaf: guarding the Bolshevik headquarters at the Smolny Institute, October 1917

While Lenin stood at the head of the party, up to the year 1923, the Bolsheviks enjoyed full freedom of inner-party debate; and Lenin was not the man to victimize any of his numerous inner-party critics and opponents.

In January 1924 Lenin died; and immediately there was bitter strife and controversy about who should succeed him. The troika or triumvirate – Stalin, Zinoviev and Kamenev – were determined to exclude Trotsky from the succession. At this stage, oddly enough, Zinoviev rather than Stalin came forward as Trotsky's worst enemy, demanding his expulsion from the party: Stalin was against expulsion. Some time later, after he had fallen out with Zinoviev and Kamenev, Stalin said:

Stalin: Comrades, our differences with Zinoviev and Kamenev began with the question: What is to be done with Trotsky? That was towards the end of 1924. Zinoviev and his friends urged us to expel Trotsky from the party. But we, that is the majority of the Central Committee, we did not agree with this. (APPLAUSE.) After some altercation, we persuaded Zinoviev and his friends to withdraw this demand. But some time later, at a full session of the Central Committee, Zinoviev and Kamenev again demanded of us that we should at once expel Trotsky from the party. And again we refused. We refused because we thought that such chopping-off of heads might become very dangerous. Comrades, this method of chopping off and blood-letting – and, mind you, Zinoviev and Kamenev cried out for Trotsky's blood – this method is dangerous and contagious. Today they chop off one head, tomorrow another and the day after tomorrow still another – who in the end will be left with us in the party?

What moved Stalin, of all people, to utter this warning? In Moscow, a story went round that, shortly after Lenin's death, the Bolshevik chiefs met and took a secret oath never to fight each other as the Jacobins did and never to guillotine each other. Whether the story was true or not, it is a fact that for a long time Lenin's successors felt bound by the rule that no party member should ever be punished with death for any political offence. The G.P.U., the political police, were not allowed to lay hands on any communist unless the Central Committee authorized them to do so.

And so, for years, the inner-party struggle went on bloodlessly, even though its vehemence grew continuously. The Jacobin ghosts haunted the Bolsheviks. Thus the inner Bolshevik struggles dragged on for thirteen or fourteen years, from 1923 till 1936, before Stalin put the guillotine in action. Note that all the struggles within the Jacobin party were fought out within a few months only.

Yet even in the middle of the 1920s the division in the Bolshevik Party already looked ominously like those in the Jacobin party. There was the Left opposition led by Trotsky, with ultra-radical groups such as the Workers' Opposition in the background; the Right, led by Bukharin and Rykov; and the Centre, with Stalin at its head. In the summer of 1927 Stalin attacked Trotsky, Zinoviev and Kamenev – the last two had in the meantime become Trotsky's allies – and arraigned them before the Central Control Commission, the party's supreme tribunal. Now it was Stalin who demanded that Trotsky and his friends should be expelled from the Central Committee. On 24 July Trotsky was replying to Stalin's charges. This was a tense day for Red Moscow. There was much commotion in the lobbies of the Central Committee and the Central Control Commission, for the party tribunal was still reluctant to act on Stalin's prompting. A veteran Bolshevik, Solz, was to preside over the tribunal. Just before the opening of the proceedings he talked with Vorobiev, one of Trotsky's followers.

Solz: Do you know what the opposition's latest Manifesto amounts to? Do you know, Vorobiev, what this leads to? Surely you know the history of the French revolution? And you should remember what this kind of action led to in Paris – to arrests and to the guillotine!

Vorobiev (VERY ASSURED): Is it your intention then, comrade Solz, is it your intention to arrest and to guillotine us members of the opposition?

Solz: But, Vorobiev, this does not depend on our intentions. We shall be sorry if things come to this pass; but they may and they will come to this, if you go on behaving as you do. Do you suppose that Robespierre was not sorry for Danton when he sent him to the guillotine? And yet he did it; and then Robespierre had to go himself. Do you think he was not sorry? But he had to do it – he had to.

When Trotsky came forward to make his plea, he referred to that conversation between Solz and Vorobiev.

Trotsky: In my opinion, comrade Solz was right to draw this analogy with the French revolution. Today we must at all costs brush up our knowledge of the great French revolution. During that revolution, many were guillotined. We too had many people brought before the firing squad. But there were two distinct chapters in the history of the French revolution, the chapter of its rise and the chapter of its decline. We must understand this. When the line went like this, upwards, the French Jacobins, the Bolsheviks of that age, guillotined the Royalists and the Girondins. We had a similar great chapter. It was when we Oppositionists, together with you, shot the White Guards and exiled our Girondins, the Mensheviks. But then there began in France that other chapter, when the Thermidorians began shooting the Left Jacobins – I would like comrade Solz to think over this analogy, to think it through to the end, and to give himself the answer to the following question: which chapter of the revolution is this – that of ascent, or that of decline – in which chapter is Solz

Left: Kamenev with Lenin in 1922. Opposite page: portrait of Trotsky by Annenkov

Lenin's body is carried to lie in state at the Hall of Columns in Moscow, by Bukharin, Rykov, Mikoyan, Molotov, Stalin, Zinoviev and Tomsky

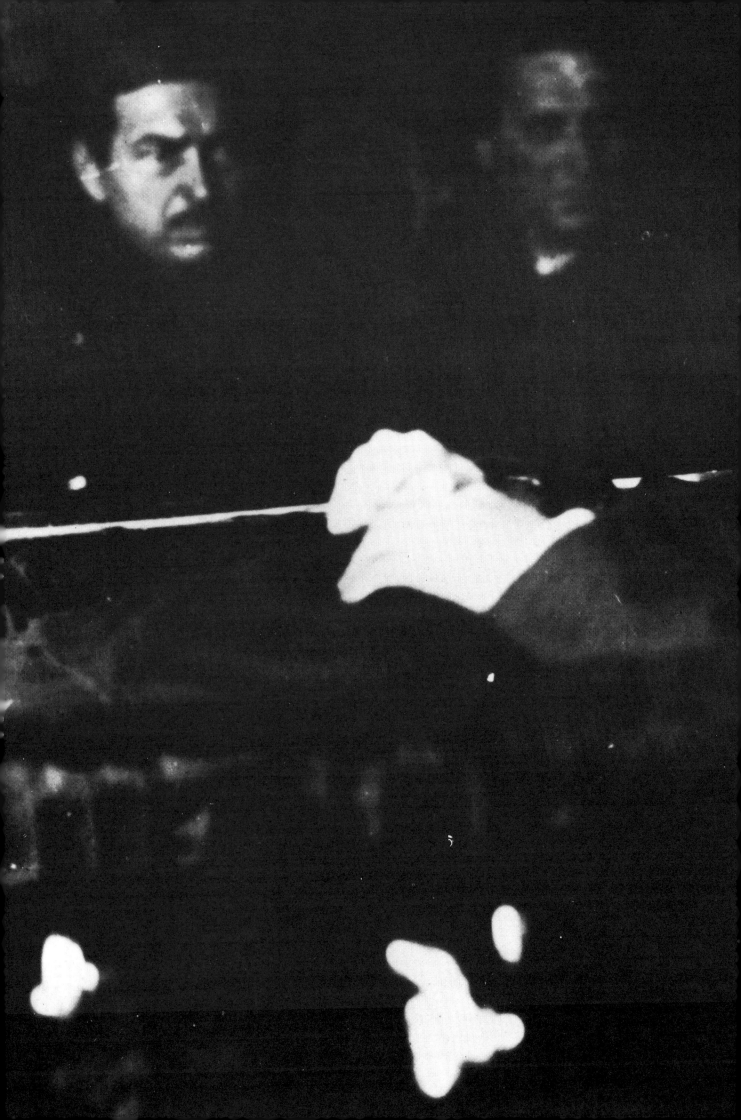

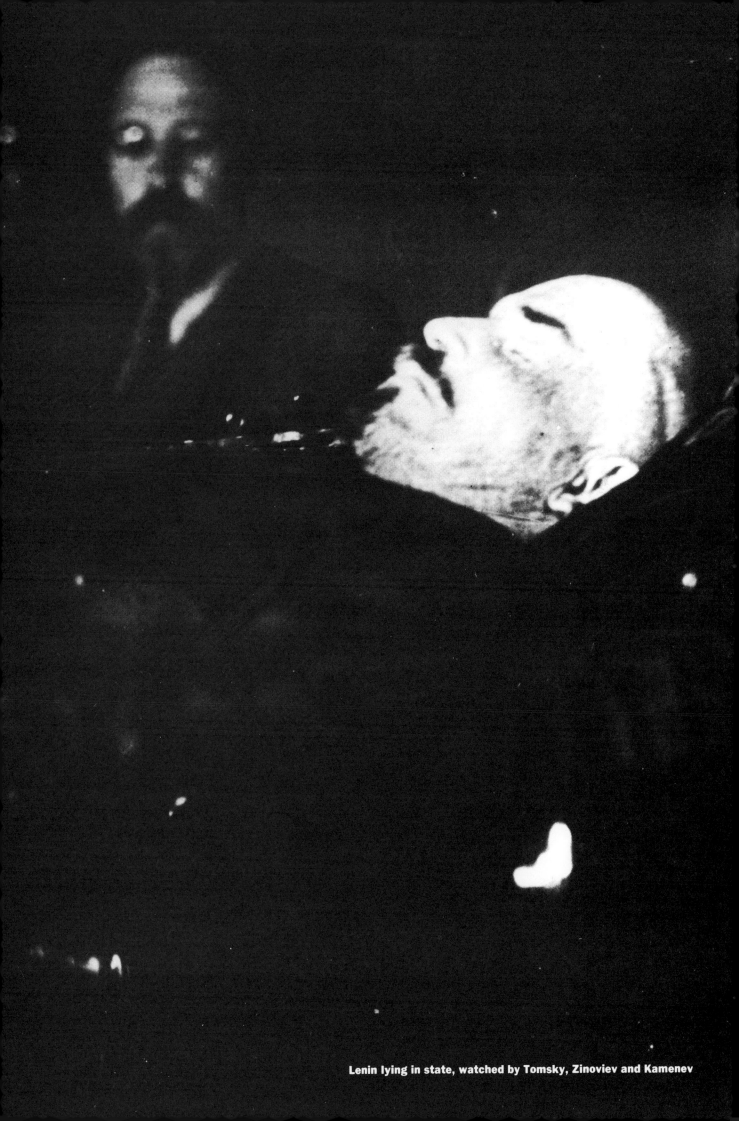

Lenin lying in state, watched by Tomsky, Zinoviev and Kamenev

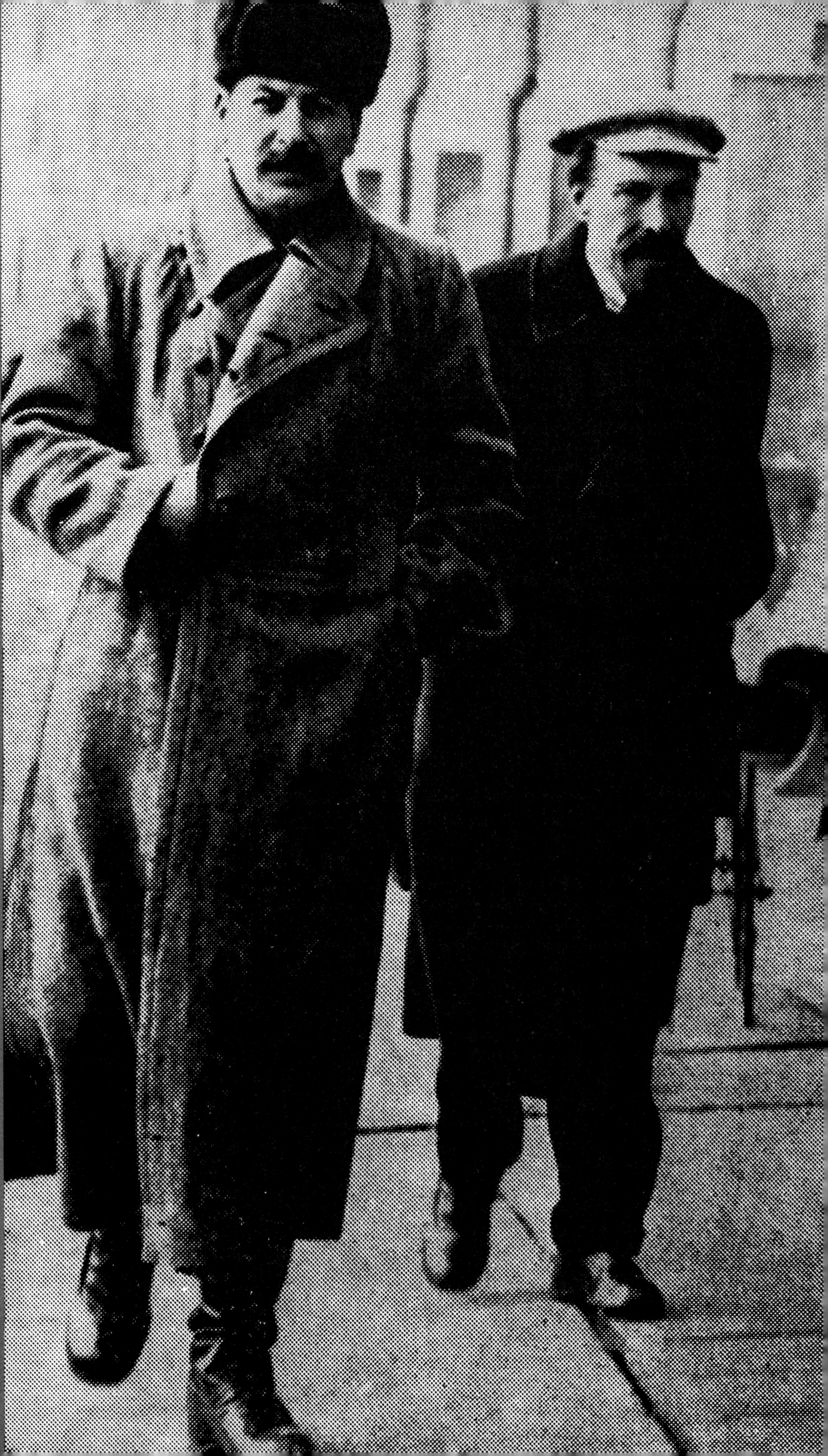

Lenin's heirs: Stalin, Rykov, Kamenev and Zinoviev

Red Week, 1924: left to right, Voroshilov, Trotsky, Kalinin, Frunze (with Budienny above him) and Clara Zetkin taking the salute on Lenin's mausoleum

1926: the funeral of Felix Dzerzhinsky, founder of the CHEKA. Rykov is second from left, with Trotsky behind him; Stalin is dressed in white; Bukharin is on the extreme right. This was Trotsky's last official appearance in Russia

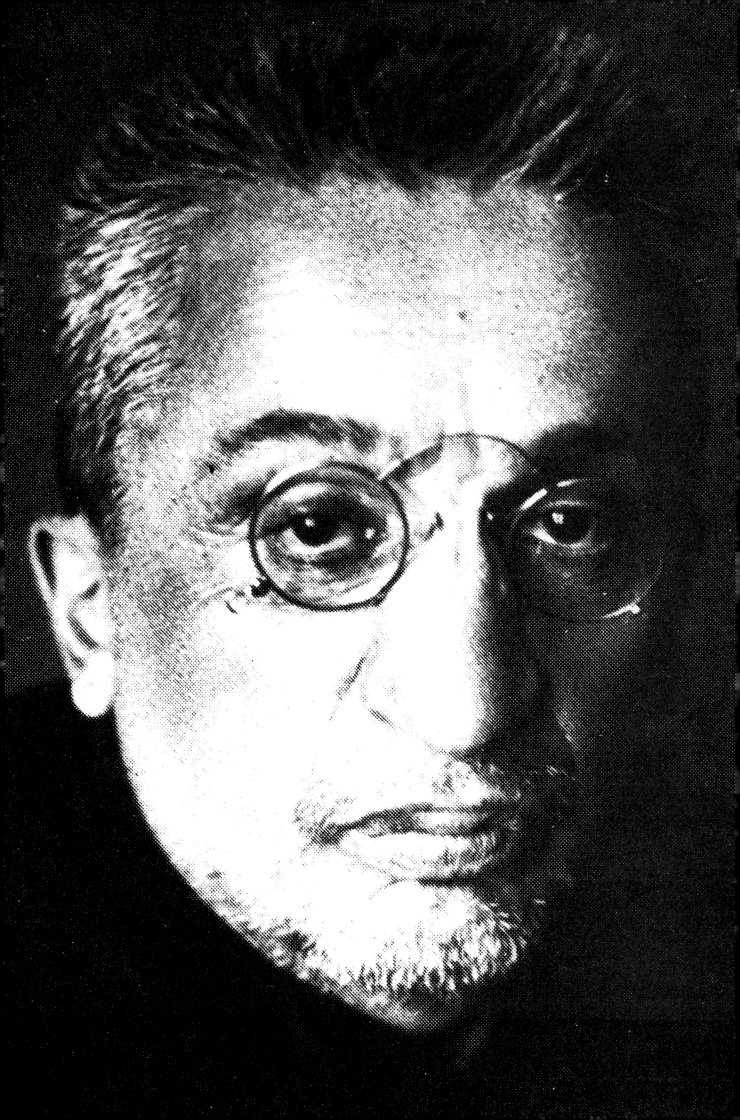

preparing to have us shot? (COMMOTION IN THE HALL, PROTESTS, JEERS.) This is no jesting matter. Revolution is a serious business. None of us is scared of a firing squad. We are all old revolutionists. But, comrade Solz, this is the Thermidorian chapter. (UPROAR IN THE HALL.) When we speak about Thermidorians, this is taken as a term of abuse. You imagine that the Thermidorians were arrant counter-revolutionaries, conscious monarchists and so on. They were nothing of the kind. They were still Jacobins, but Jacobins who had moved to the right. The Jacobin organization had arrived at the conviction that it was necessary to destroy the Robespierre group. Do you think that on the very next day after the coup of the 9th Thermidor, they said to themselves: we have now transferred power into the hands of the bourgeoisie? Nothing of the kind. Look up the newspapers of that time. The Thermidorians said: we have destroyed a small group of people who disrupted peace in the party and now, after their destruction,

the revolution will triumph completely. If comrade Solz has any doubts about it . . .

Solz: You are practically repeating my own words.

Trotsky: So much the better, comrade Solz. It will help us considerably if we are agreed on this. Let me read to you what Brival, a right-wing Jacobin, a Thermidorian, said when he reported on that session of the Convention during which Robespierre and the other Jacobins were handed over to the Revolutionary Tribunal. That is what Brival said: 'Intriguers and counter-revolutionists, covering themselves with togas of patriotism – they aimed at the destruction of Liberty. The Convention ordered them placed under arrest. Those arrested were Robespierre, Couton, Saint-Just, Lebas and Robespierre the Younger. The Chairman asked what my opinion was. I replied: 'Those who have always voted in accordance with the principles of the Jacobins, those vote for the arrest.' I did even more than that – I am one of those who proposed

this measure. Moreover, as Secretary, I made haste to sign and transmit this decree of the Convention.' This is how a Solz of that age made his report. Robespierre and his associates – these were described as the counter-revolutionaries, just as we are being described here. 'Those who always voted in accordance with Jacobin principles' signified in the language of that time 'those who have always been Bolsheviks'. As Secretary, said he, I made haste to sign and transmit the Convention's decree about Robespierre's arrest. Today too there are Secretaries who make haste to sign and transmit – today too there are such Secretaries.

The audience grasped the hint: Stalin was the party's General Secretary.

Trotsky: Listen further, comrades, to this manifesto to France, which the Convention issued after the annihilation of Robespierre, Saint-Just and others: '*Citoyens*, amid the brilliant victories over foreign armies the Republic is

Trotsky speaking at Adolf Yoffe's funeral in November 1927 — his last speech in Russia. Opposite page: Aaron Solz

threatened by a new danger. The work of the Convention would be barren, and the courage of our armies would be purposeless, if you, citizens, were to waver in your choice between France and a few isolated individuals. Obey the call of the country! Do not join the ranks of evil-minded aristocrats and of enemies of the people – save France!' They thought that only a few isolated individuals stood in the way of the triumph of the revolution. They did not understand that those 'isolated' individuals reflected the innermost revolutionary forces and impulses of that time, the forces that resisted the revolution's decline and degeneration into Bonapartism. The Thermidorians appealed to the people, 'Obey the call of France! Do not join those evil-minded men!' They denounced Robespierre and his friends as aristocrats. And did we not hear today the very same cry – 'aristocrat' addressed to me by one of the judges. I have been described as an accomplice of Austen Chamberlain, the British Foreign Secretary. I could quote to you any number of statements denouncing the revolutionary Jacobins as agents of Pitt, the Austen Chamberlain of that time. The analogies are truly startling. This is Aulard, the historian of the French revolution. 'Robespierre's enemies were not content with killing him and his friends. They slandered them, and presented them to France as Royalists and foreign mercenaries.' And does not *Pravda* today begin to slander us in the same way? From the leading article in today's *Pravda* our nostrils detect the odour of the second chapter, the odour of decline. That odour is penetrating the official institutions of our party. Our inner-party regime stifles all who struggle against the re-enactment of Thermidor. In the party, the ordinary worker has been stifled, the rank and file is silent. You are calling for a new purge, and you wish the party to be silent. Such is our party regime. Let us recall again the history of the Jacobin clubs. They had two kinds of purges there. When the wave went upwards, the moderates were ejected from the Jacobin clubs. When the line began to curve downwards, the revolutionaries, the Left Jacobins, were expelled. How did this affect the Jacobin clubs? An anonymous regime of terror was instituted. Silence was made compulsory. A hundred-per-cent vote and abstention from all criticism were demanded. It was obligatory to think in

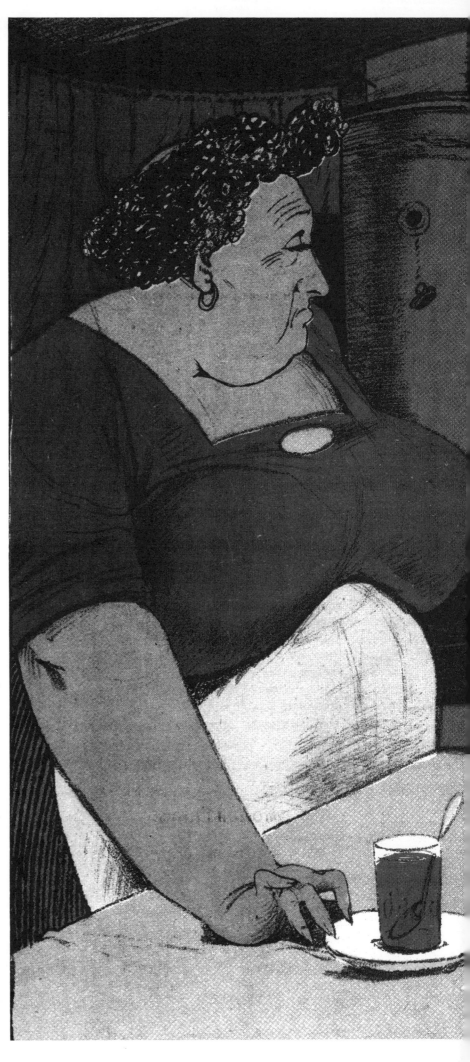

accordance with orders from above. Men were compelled to give up the idea that the party is a living independent organism, and not a self-sufficient machine of power. And so, the Jacobin clubs, the crucibles of the revolution, became the nurseries of the Napoleonic bureaucracy of the future. By all means let us learn from the French revolution; but must we repeat it? (SHOUTS AND UPROAR.) I am not jesting here. No one, for the sake of mere trifles, would run risks as grave as those that we are taking. I do not know whether this is my last opportunity to address you here. I am not using the time allotted to me simply to refute miserable charges, but to pose basic questions. Beware of what you are doing. There is no need to rush. There is no need to take decisions that cannot be reversed. Beware of having one day to confess: we parted company with those whom we should have preserved, while preserving those from whom we should have parted.

Four months later, in December 1927, the Fifteenth Party Congress assembled in Moscow. The leaders of the opposition had already been expelled, and Stalin thus sought to justify the act:
Stalin: Why has the party expelled Trotsky and Zinoviev? Because they are the ringleaders of the opposition. (HEAR, HEAR!) Because they got the idea that no one would dare touch them, because they wanted to create for themselves a privileged position in the party. But we do not want aristocrats in our party who enjoy privileges while peasants are deprived of these privileges. Is it to be thought that we Bolsheviks, who have destroyed the aristocracy root and branch, that we will now restore it in our own party? (APPLAUSE.) You want to know why we have expelled Trotsky and Zinoviev from the party? Because we want no aristocrats; because we have one law for all. (HEAR, HEAR!

Left: drawing by Eliseev, published in Krokodil in November 1927, caricaturing Zinoviev as a housewife, Trotsky as an irate husband and Kamenev as a little boy sitting on Trotsky's knee.
Overleaf: Rykov (with camera) and Bukharin at the 15th Party Congress in Moscow, December 1927

PROLONGED APPLAUSE!) If the opposition wants to remain in the party, let them submit to the will of the party. If they do not want that, let them find a better place for themselves. (HEAR, HEAR!) We put only one condition to the opposition: they must disarm, disarm entirely and completely. (PROLONGED APPLAUSE.) They must sincerely and vehemently discard their anti-Bolshevik views, and so that the whole world may hear. (HEAR, HEAR! PROLONGED APPLAUSE.) They must denounce the mistakes they have committed – mistakes that have turned into crimes against the party. They must sincerely and vehemently denounce them so that the whole world may hear. (HEAR, HEAR! PROLONGED APPLAUSE.) Either they do this, or they clear out. And if they do not clear out, we will kick them out. (HEAR, HEAR! PROLONGED APPLAUSE.)

Expulsion from the party was the first penalty Stalin inflicted on his opponents. The next was to imprison them or deport them to Siberia. He did not yet demand capital punishment. The purges were still bloodless. Stalin himself was still afraid of chopping off heads. But he was even more afraid of the heads he had not chopped off. Even from prison and exile, still his enemies propagated their views, still they were critical of him. Not yet daring to kill them off, he pressed them to commit moral suicide. He demanded that they should recant their own views – denounce their own mistakes. Cromwell and Robespierre too had occasionally sought to extract a recantation from a defeated opponent; but only occasionally. In the Russian Purges, recantation is a regular and essential feature.

Let us return to the year 1927, to see how these Russian recantations began. Many of Stalin's communist critics were terrified by the thought that, if they persisted in the struggle against him, they might as the Jacobins had done, bring doom upon themselves, the party and the revolution. They yielded to Stalin, they surrendered and recanted, hoping to keep the guillotine at bay and to gain time. At the Fifteenth Congress, after Stalin had called the leaders of the opposition to repent 'in the hearing of the whole world', the opposition split. Trotsky and his friends refused to repent, while Kamenev, Zinoviev and their followers announced their surrender and made their first recantation. This is Kamenev addressing the Congress:

Kamenev: Comrades, I am appearing on this platform only in order to find a path leading to peace between the opposition and the party. The struggle that has been going on these past years has become so acute that all of us have now to choose between two possible roads. One possibility open to us would be to set up another party. But this would be ruinous for the revolution; we cannot choose this road. Our own views and Lenin's teaching rule this out altogether. Hence only the other road is open to us, the road of a complete and thorough capitulation to the party. After a fierce, and bitter, and obstinate struggle for our views, we are surrendering, because we are deeply convinced that a correct Leninist policy can be made to triumph only in and through our party, not outside it or despite it. We have decided to submit, and to carry out all decisions of the Congress, no matter how hard these may be on us.

Packed by Stalin's men, the Congress replied with howls of derision and mockery. Kamenev still tried to save his own dignity and that of his political friends.

Kamenev: In surrendering to Congress we act as Bolsheviks. But if you were to ask us alone to renounce our views, then you would ask us to act in an un-Bolshevik manner. Comrades, never before has anyone in our party been asked to repudiate his own views. If we were to renounce the views we advocated only a week or a fortnight ago, that would be hypocrisy on our part, and you would not believe us.

(SHOUTS FROM THE FLOOR: 'THIS IS A VILE MANOEUVRE', 'TRICKSTER', LAUGHTER AND DERISION.)

Comrades, give us at least a chance to

prove our sincerity . . .

The commotion in the hall grew louder as Kamenev went on to ask that imprisoned members of the opposition, Trotskyists and Zinovievists, should be released.

Stalin: I will not deal with comrade Kamenev's speech. It was the most hypocritical, pharisaical, crafty and rascally of all the opposition speeches delivered from this platform. (HEAR, HEAR! APPLAUSE.)

Congress declared that it did not accept Kamenev's and Zinoviev's statements of surrender. Alexei Rykov was still Soviet Prime Minister and leader of the right wing of the party, now acting in coalition with the Stalinist centre. He addressed the Congress:

Rykov: Comrades, Kamenev concluded his speech with the declaration that he did not dissociate himself from the imprisoned members of the opposition. I should begin my speech with this statement: I do not dissociate myself from those members of our party who have put some of these oppositionists into prison. (TUMULTUOUS APPLAUSE. SHOUTS OF 'HURRAY!') I think we shall have to put behind bars quite a few more of the oppositionists. (SHOUTS OF 'HURRAY!'. 'LONG LIVE THE LENINIST CENTRAL COMMITTEE!' THE DELEGATES RISE AND APPLAUD RYKOV.)

According to Kamenev, the demand that people should repudiate their own views has never before been made in our party. He claims that we have no right to make such a demand on the opposition. But Kamenev and his associates have gone out into the streets and called for the overthrow of the Central Committee.

(VOICES: 'Shame!')

Yes, they have called for the overthrow of the Central Committee – this was an open challenge to the Soviet government. (HEAR, HEAR! APPLAUSE.) The danger threatening us from Kamenev and his associates is a thousand times greater than the danger from any opposition our party has ever before had to face. Under Lenin the party would never have allowed such outrageous, such unheard-of, anti-Soviet actions. Comrade Kamenev, you and your friends belong to Trotsky's illegal party. In the name of the revolution, why do you not withdraw from it. Not one of us here believes that you really say what you are thinking. Both you and Trotsky have been active in politics for twenty-five or thirty years. Can you really not understand that by arousing street demonstrations against us, you were preparing and organizing a *coup d'état*? (HEAR, HEAR!) If you had succeeded with these demonstrations, if some tens of thousands or a hundred thousand people had responded to your call, there would have been street fighting in Leningrad and Moscow, wouldn't there? (HEAR, HEAR!) That would be civil war.

A few years later Rykov himself was to be in conflict with Stalin, and was to make his own recantation. Meanwhile, after Congress had refused to accept Zinoviev's and Kamenev's surrender, Zinoviev and Kamenev met Trotsky for the last time to discuss their tactics. Trotsky was adamant against any surrender. Nothing was more alien to his character than recantation. He had not even asked to be admitted to the party Congress to plead his cause. He was determined to go on with his struggle, come what might.

On 18 December 1927 Zinoviev and Kamenev carried their surrender a step further and renounced their own views, as Congress had asked them to do.

Here is Trotsky venting his contempt for the 'capitulators'.

Trotsky: These are dead souls. If Stalin, like Gogol's hero, wishes to collect dead souls, let him do so. We have nothing in common with them.

Zinoviev and Kamenev had hoped to be able to pronounce their recantation from the rostrum of the Congress; but they were not admitted to the Congress hall. Bukharin and Rykov went out to talk to them.

Opposite page: left to right, Lashevich, Frunze, Smirnov, Rykov, Voroshilov, Stalin, Skrypnik, Bubnov and Ordjonikidze in April 1925. Right: the same photograph published 14 years later, retouched and rearranged to suggest that the group only included Frunze, Voroshilov, Stalin and Ordjonikidze, thereby erasing the other five from history

Rykov (front left) and Stalin (front right) voting with party cards at the 15th Congress

Left Oppositionists, exiled to Siberia,
demonstrate on the anniversary of the revolution in 1928.
The banner on the left bears the slogan
'Turn the fire to the Right, against Kulak, Nepman and
Bureaucrat, not in words but in deeds';
that in the centre, with portraits of Lenin and Trotsky, proclaims
'Long Live the Dictatorship of the Proletariat'

Bukharin: You have done well to make up your mind. This was the last moment. The iron curtain of history is just coming down.

The iron curtain that was presently to crush Bukharin and Rykov as well.

Rykov: About noon today I received this statement of recantation from Kamenev, but I refused to grant his request and to allow him to come in here and read this statement, and address Congress in person. I told him that I had no right to admit him because he and his comrades had been expelled from the party – (HEAR, HEAR!) lest anyone should ever again imagine that he could do again what the opposition has done. (STORMY APPLAUSE.)

While Congress was refusing to accept even this recantation or to re-instate Zinoviev and Kamenev, the unrepentant oppositionists were being deported from Moscow – Trotsky to Alma Ata on the Chinese frontier, others to Siberia and to the sub-Polar regions. Zinoviev was ordered to take up temporary residence at Voronezh, not far from Moscow. Kamenev was allowed to stay in the capital. Even now Stalin did not dare to set the guillotine in motion. Ordjonikidze, Stalin's country-man, who tabled the motion for the expulsion of the opposition, stated at the Congress:

Ordjonikidze: Comrades, we are well aware of the tremendous significance of the decision submitted to you. We all know only too well how hard it is to expel from the party men who have brought a good deal of benefit to the party, and who have, for many years, fought in our ranks. But they have compelled us to do it – I repeat, they have compelled us.

Note the curious parallelism of development, in France and in Russia. Robespierre, one remembers, defeated the Jacobin Left, the Hébertists and men of the Commune, with the help of the Dantonists, the Jacobin Right. Stalin similarly defeated the Left Opposition, the Trotskyists and the Zinovievists, with the help of the right-wing Bolsheviks, Bukharin, Rykov and Tomsky. And like Robespierre, Stalin almost at once turned against his erstwhile allies on the Right. At the beginning of the year 1928, while the Trotskyists were being deported from Moscow, a new split was already developing in the Politbureau and the Central Committee; Stalin was turning against the kulak, in fact against the peasant smallholder at large. Bukharin, Rykov and Tomsky defended the peasantry. For some time the outcome was undecided; but Stalin worked hard to eliminate the Bukharinists from positions of power and influence. In the summer of 1928, the two factions were already at daggers drawn. In July, only six months after Trotsky's deportation, Bukharin was already trying to make common cause against Stalin with the Trotskyists and the Zinovievists whom he had just helped to defeat. As we have already seen he secretly approached

Left to right: Yaroslavsky, Kaganovich, Ordjonikidze, Voroshilov, Stalin, Andreev and Molotov.
Overleaf: May Day in Red Square, Moscow, 1928

Kamenev with this proposal.

But nothing came of it. When Stalin learned about Bukharin's and Kamenev's secret meeting he raised the matter at the Politbureau; and Bukharin replied with panicky and tearful apologies. Even at this late stage, Stalin did not dare to take the lives of his opponents; but as a precaution he banished Trotsky from Russia. And in the next few years, Bukharin's terrified whisper at his meeting with Kamenev – he will slay us – he will strangle us – echoed in the ears of all anti-Stalinists throughout the Soviet Union.

"Shoot The Mad Dogs..."

The 1930s in the Soviet Union began amid tremendous turmoil. Stalin had just decreed the so-called liquidation of the kulaks – in fact the dispossession of twenty-four million peasants, and the forcible collectivization of their farms. The countryside became the theatre of undeclared civil war. The peasants tenaciously clung to their property, attacked and killed party commissars, slaughtered cattle, burned barns and stables, and buried or destroyed whole harvests of grain. The G.P.U. replied with mass executions and mass deportations. Mammoth concentration camps were set up in the enormous desolate plains of Siberia and in the icy wastes of the Far North.

Yet in these terrible years, years of starvation and famine, the Soviet Union also laid the foundations of its new economic power. The cities and towns worked in a fever of industrial expansion. New steel mills and factories were

built, new coalmines and oilfields were sunk, new armament plants were erected. Production of consumer goods was deliberately neglected; and the industrial drive became a nation-wide scramble for scarce materials and for labour. Millions of dispossessed peasants were forced into the towns, crowded into huge barracks, kept under military discipline, trained in industrial skills and brought to the factory benches. In one decade, the urban population rose from thirty million to sixty million. Barefoot, tattered, hungry and homeless workers were turning Russia into one of the world's leading industrial powers. Disease, drunkenness and industrial disasters took a heavy toll. Peter the Great built St Petersburg on the marshes and the bones of Russia's serfs; Stalin built not just one city but the whole might of modern Russia on the bones and blood of millions of workers and peasants.

Engaged in this colossal undertaking, Stalin did his best to arouse the enthusiasm of the young for the magnitude of the tasks assigned to them. He stirred up national ambition and pride. He invoked the vision of the socialist society of the future; in its name he called for sacrifice and popular heroism. But he also had to suppress popular anger, despair and resentment. He employed stupendous, all-pervading terror; and watched with sleepless vigilance over the security of his personal power. The cult of his personality was established. He was hailed as the benefactor of all Soviet peoples, the builder of socialism, the fount of all wisdom, the supreme judge, in all matters of national and international life. No one dared to challenge his authority, not even by hint or by allusion. He turned the atheistic state founded by Lenin into a church of

his own, Stalinist, cult. All his former colleagues, comrades and rivals had to kow-tow to him. At every party congress the leaders of the oppositions, Zinoviev, Kamenev, Bukharin, Rykov, Tomsky and others, were coming forward with ever new recantations – and with ever new panegyrics of Stalin. The abjectness of these performances was matched only by their nauseating monotony. Even Trotsky's former friends (Radek, Preobrazhensky, Ivan Smirnov, Rakovsky, Muralov and others), men who had once held the highest positions in party and state and had since spent years in Stalin's prisons and places of exile, were at last prevailed upon to abjure their views, to surrender and to join in the parades of Stalinist servility.

These were some of the most gloomy and puzzling events in modern Russian history. What caused all these men to prostrate themselves? There is no simple answer. Some broke down under the relentless terror to which they themselves and their next-of-kin were subjected. Others came to doubt the wisdom of their opposition to Stalin. Still others, anxious to play their part in the industrialization of the Soviet Union, swallowed their pride in order to regain a place in Soviet society. And since they were all communists devoted to their party and state, they were terrified by the thought that their revolution, and their party, might be heading for disaster. Amid the turmoil of collectivization, that danger appeared real enough. Then came Hitler's rise to power, and his call to an anti-Soviet crusade. In these circumstances many of Stalin's communist opponents decided to put a stop to the inner-party struggle, even though they had to do this on Stalin's humiliating terms.

Above left: peasants carrying a banner with the inscription 'We demand collectivisation and the liquidation of the kulaks as a class'.
Opposite page: Stalin in December 1929

The fabrication of the Stalin myth:
the photograph above of Lenin and Stalin in Gorki in 1922
bears every sign of having been faked at a later
date to exaggerate the closeness of their relationship.
Opposite: the sculpture called
'Lenin and Stalin in Gorki' was commissioned in 1939
when Stalin had supreme power —
one of thousands like it throughout the Soviet Union

В кругу слева направо — Я. М. СВЕРДЛОВ, Л. Д. ТРОЦКИЙ, Г. Е. ЗИНОВЬЕВ, И. В. СТАЛИН, Л. Б. КАМЕНЕВ, М. С. УРИЦКИЙ, А. С. БУБНОВ, Г. Я. СОКОЛЬНИКОВ, Ф. Э. ДЗЕРЖИНСКИЙ. За кругом 1-й ряд снизу — В. П. НОГИН, В. П. МИЛЮТИН. 2-й ряд — А. А. ИОФФЕ, Н. Н. КРЕСТИНСКИЙ. 3-й ряд — И. Т. СМИЛГА, АРТЕМ (Ф. А. СЕРГЕЕВ). 4-й ряд — Е. Д. СТАСОВА, А. ЛОМОВ (Г. И. ОППОКОВ), А. И. РЫКОВ, Н. И. БУХАРИН, С. Г. ШАУМЯН, А. М. КОЛЛОНТАЙ

The Bolshevik Central Committee, elected at the Sixth Congress, as represented in a montage made ten years later, in 1927. Surrounding Lenin in the circle from left to right are Sverdlov, Trotsky, Zinoviev, Stalin, Kamenev, Uritsky, Bubnov, Sokolnikov and Dzerzhinsky. Behind the circle, bottom row, Nogin and Miliutin; second row, Yoffe and Krestinsky; third row, Smilga and Sergeev; fourth row, Stasova, Lomov, Rykov, Bukharin, Shaumian and Kollontai

The same subject is given a different interpretation in 1935, after eight year's of Stalin's dominance. Stalin now comes second to Lenin, followed by Sverdlov, Bubnov, Dzerzhinsky, Shaumian, Uritsky, Muranov, Krestinsky, Miliutin, Kollontai, Sergeev, Sokolnikov, Bukharin, Rykov, Berzin, Nogin, Kamenev, Zinoviev, Trotsky and Smilga. Many of those who had been in the Bolshevik inner circle at the time of the revolution are here portrayed as relatively unimportant

Only one man, the banished Trotsky, continued to challenge Stalin. From his various places of exile in Turkey, France and Norway, he ceaselessly attacked the Moscow dictator. His voice did not penetrate to the masses in Russia; but it reached the men of the Bolshevik hierarchy – the Trotskyists, Zinovievists, Bukharinists and even the old Stalinist cadres, who listened intently to every word uttered by the founder of the Red Army. In Bolshevik eyes, Trotsky still represented the sole alternative to Stalin and Stalinism; and so the whole Stalinist propaganda machine concentrated immense efforts upon discrediting him. Trotsky was: 'The spearhead of the world's counter-revolution.' 'A social fascist!' 'Just say, a fascist!' 'A plotter and conspirator against the Soviet Union!' He was indeed the devil, or the anti-Christ, of the Stalinist cult.

Stalin compelled Trotsky's erstwhile friends and followers to join him in exorcizing the devil. Yet the exorcisms were losing their magical power. The U.S.S.R. existed in a state of almost permanent emergency. In 1932 Nadia Alliluyeva, Stalin's wife, committed suicide in protest against the monstrosities of his rule. The oppositionists who had surrendered to Stalin came to regret the surrender; and even in his own entourage there was no lack of malcontents. And so Stalin was becoming afraid not only of Trotskyists, Bukharinists, etc., but even of his own followers, the Stalinists.

The higher he rose, and the more grotesquely he was adulated, the louder grew the murmurs around him, the more numerous was the multitude who had reason to fear and hate him – and whom he feared and hated. Though elevated above the whole Bolshevik Party, it was not without reason that he saw the whole party as one potential coalition against himself. And he had to use every ounce of his strength and cunning to prevent the potential from becoming actual. He had not obtained mastery once and for all. He had to obtain it over and over again. On 1 December 1934, a young communist by the name of Nikolayev assassinated Sergei Kirov, the party boss and Governor of Leningrad. The exact circumstances in which this event took place are still obscure. What was known at the time was that the chiefs of the Leningrad G.P.U. had been aware of

Nadia Stalin lying in state, Moscow, 1932

Below: Kirov (second from left) at
Nadia Stalin's funeral.
Opposite page: left to right, Molotov,
Voroshilov, Stalin and Kalinin carrying
the urn containing Kirov's ashes.
Overleaf: The original caption to this
photograph reads,
"Death to the traitors - Stalin signs
a death warrant, 1933".
Kossior looks on

Nikolayev's preparations for the attempt and that, either deliberately or negligently, they had allowed him to carry out the coup. Khrushchev has since hinted that Stalin may have connived at the crime. Whatever the truth, Stalin at once exploited Kirov's assassination for his own political purposes. He accused Zinoviev and Kamenev of being responsible – he had them expelled, for the third time, from the party; he had them imprisoned and court-martialled. Zinoviev and Kamenev at first declared that they had had no dealings with the assassin. Then, after much grilling, they admitted that the assassin *might* have

been influenced by their *past* criticisms of Stalin – past, not present or even recent, criticisms. Stalin's propaganda-machine at once seized upon this ambiguous, semi-admission. Zinoviev and Kamenev, and their followers, were accused of incitement to subversion and terror. The two men were sentenced to imprisonment for ten and five years respectively. Trotsky was denounced as the chief instigator of all the crimes with which the opposition was charged. At once terror was let loose on an unprecedented scale. Many thousands of so-called 'assassins of Kirov' were sent from Leningrad to concentration camps.

A special decree empowered the G.P.U. to treat the relatives of any so-called traitor as himself being guilty of treason; and so not only genuine Trotskyists or Zinovievists, and those suspected of associating with them, but also their wives, parents and even children, were similarly deported.

The campaign against 'Kirov's assassins' had been running for about twenty months, when suddenly, on 15 August 1936, Moscow announced that a trial of 'the Trotskyite–Zinovievite Terrorist Centre' was about to open. This was to be the first of the great and infamous Moscow trials. Sixteen men were put

Andrei Vyshinsky, Chief Prosecutor.
Opposite page: courtroom scene
of a political trial in Moscow, 1930

into the dock: Zinoviev, Kamenev, Yevdokimov, Bakayev, Mrachkovsky, Ter-Vaganyan, Ivan Smirnov and others. These were old Bolsheviks, heroes of the civil war. Smirnov had defeated Kolchak's white armies in Siberia. Mrachkovsky had distinguished himself on the battlefield by feats of almost legendary courage. On the other hand, Counsel for the Prosecution was Andrey Vyshinsky, who had been a right-wing Menshevik bitterly opposed to the October revolution and who had not climbed upon the Bolshevik bandwaggon until after the civil war.

The Trial of the Sixteen, as this trial came to be called, took place before the Military Tribunal of the Supreme Court in Moscow. Nominally it was an open trial. But night and day, without a break, interrogators had for weeks been grilling and conditioning the defendants. Zinoviev and Kamenev, already sentenced and imprisoned for bearing an *indirect* moral responsibility for Kirov's assassination, were now tried again under the charge of *direct* responsibility. They were also accused of having on Trotsky's orders prepared attempts on the lives of Stalin, Voroshilov, Kaganovich, Ordjonikidze, Zhdanov, Kossior and Postyshev – all members of the Politbureau. Listen to Vyshinsky as he delivers the indictment:

Vyshinsky: It now transpires that eighteen months ago, when they investigated comrade S. M. Kirov's assassination, the judicial authorities still lacked evidence that would fully reveal the true roles of Zinoviev, of Kamenev, of their friends – and of the clandestine Trotskyist organization. New facts have come to light, some of them connected with a number of Trotskyist and Zinovievist clandestine groups. On these bases, the prosecution can now prove as follows: Zinoviev, Kamenev, Yevdokimov and Bakayev not only knew that their adherents in Leningrad were inclined towards terrorist acts; they themselves really were the direct organizers of comrade S. M. Kirov's assassination. The prosecution has now further established that Zinoviev and his followers pursued their criminal activities in direct understanding with the Trotskyists and with Leon Trotsky himself, who is at present out of the country. At the end of the year 1932 they united their organizations under a single directing centre on which Zinoviev, Kamenev, Yevdokimov and Bakayev represented their faction, while I. N. Smirnov, Ter-

Vaganyan and Mrachkovsky represented the Trotskyists. They formed special terrorist squads, whose task it was to assassinate comrades Stalin, Voroshilov, Kaganovich, Kirov, Zhdanov, Kossior, Ordjonikidze, Postyshev and others.

Vyshinsky quoted at length the defendants' previous admissions of guilt; then he proceeded with his cross-examination. Listen to Kamenev's deposition, and the questions Vyshinsky put to him:
Kamenev: I, Kamenev, together with Zinoviev and Trotsky, organized and guided this terrorist conspiracy. My motives? I had become convinced that the party's policy – Stalin's policy – was successful and victorious – successful in the only sense in which any policy can succeed in the land of socialism: it was accepted and approved by the masses of the toilers. We, the opposition, had banked on a split in the party; but this hope had proved groundless. We had

Grigori Sokolnikov with his wife.
Opposite page: a recent photograph of the Lubianka Prison in Moscow, headquarters of the GPU, where the accused were tortured and brainwashed. The statue in front is of Felix Dzerzhinsky

also hoped to come to terms with Rykov, Bukharin and Tomsky, the leaders of the Right. But Bukharin, Rykov and Tomsky had in the meantime been removed from the party leadership ... We could no longer count on any serious domestic difficulties to allow us to overthrow Stalin's leadership ... Yet we were actuated by boundless hatred ... and by lust of power. We entered into an alliance with Trotsky's followers because Trotsky's terrorist instructions suited our own inclinations. By 1932 our conspiracy had taken shape. In the summer of that year the members of our directing centre met in our villa at Lenskoye. Those present were Zinoviev, Yevdokimov, Bakayev, Kuklin, Kareyev and myself. Zinoviev reported to us on our merger with the Trotskyists; he spoke of it as of an accomplished fact. Bakayev was put in charge of the terrorist attempts in Leningrad. In June 1934 I myself went to Leningrad to prepare our people there for the attempt on Kirov's life.
Vyshinsky: Then the assassination of Kirov was directly the work of your hands?
Kamenev: Yes, it was. And apart from the leaders of the conspiracy whom I have already mentioned, there was yet another whom we preferred to keep in reserve, and who was therefore not drawn into any practical work. I am referring to Sokolnikov.

Sokolnikov had been one of the chief organizers of the October revolution, Commissar of Finance, Soviet Ambassador in London, etc. Note how Kamenev implicates here various other important personalities, who at the time of this trial were still holding high posts in party and state. In this way a tremendous chain reaction of accusation, confession, self-accusation, trials and purges is set in motion.
Kamenev: Fearing the arrest of our directing centre, we designated a small group of people to continue the terrorist activities. Sokolnikov was one of them. Serebryakov and Radek were thought to be suitable for this purpose ... They represented, of course, the Trotskyists. I personally maintained contact with Tomsky and Bukharin ... They sympathized with us.
Vyshinsky: Defendant Kamenev, how would you yourself appraise various articles and statements which you have written, and in which you have expressed your loyalty to the party? Was all this

Kamenev (in white shirt)
at John Reed's funeral back in 1920.
Opposite page: Grigori Zinoviev

deception on your part?

Kamenev: No, it was worse than deception.

Vyshinsky: Perfidy?

Kamenev: Worse than that!

Vyshinsky: Worse than deception? Worse than perfidy? Then find a word for it. Treason?

Kamenev: You have found the word.

Vyshinsky: Defendant Zinoviev, do you confirm this?

Zinoviev: Yes, I do.

Vyshinsky: Treason? Perfidy? Double-dealing?

Zinoviev: Yes, treason, perfidy, double-dealing.

Vyshinsky: In your struggle against the leaders of our party and government, were you guided by base personal motives, by lust of power?

Kamenev: Yes, we were.

Vyshinsky: Have you then been on the side of the counter-revolution?

Kamenev: Yes, we have.

Zinoviev: After the assassination of Kirov our perfidy went to such lengths that I, Zinoviev, sent an obituary to *Pravda*. *Pravda* did not publish it. As far as I remember, Kamenev and Yev-dokimov also wrote obituaries of Kirov.

Vyshinsky: Did you arrange among yourselves that you should compose and send out these obituaries?

Zinoviev: As far as I remember, I told Kamenev that I was sending an obituary to *Pravda*, and he told me that he too would write one.

Vyshinsky: Did you recommend to Bakayev a man called Bogdan, who was assigned to carry out the attempt on comrade Stalin's life? Do you confirm that?

Zinoviev: Yes, I do.

In these trials, close relatives of the defendants appear in court to testify *for* the prosecution. This circumstance points to one of the motives of the defendants' behaviour – they evidently hoped, by their confessions, to save the lives at least of some of their next-of-kin. Here, for instance, is Safonova, Smirnov's wife, in the witness box:

Safonova: Smirnov informed us about the terrorist attempt on Stalin . . . he had received directions for it from Trotsky. One day, Mrachkovsky, returning from an official visit to Stalin, related to us, that is Smirnov and myself, his conversation with Stalin. Mrachkovsky concluded his account by saying that nothing was left to us but to kill Stalin. Smirnov wholeheartedly agreed.

Vyshinsky: Accused Smirnov, what were your relations with Safonova?

Smirnov: They were good.

Vyshinsky: Good only? Was that all?

Smirnov: We were intimately related.

Vyshinsky: Were you husband and wife?

Smirnov: Yes.

Vyshinsky: Was there any personal grudge between you?

Smirnov: No.

Apart from the defendants' self-incrimination, the prosecution produced no evidence, no documents, no papers, no verifiable facts. Day after day, the confessions and the bizarre dialogues dragged on with unrelieved monotony; the voices from the dock sounded like Vyshinsky's ghostly echoes. Were the defendants drugged or hypnotized, people wondered. They were not; but in the course of preliminary interrogations that went on for weeks and even months, the defendants had to rehearse their roles with meticulous thoroughness. In order to give their confessions a modicum of plausibility, they were from time to time allowed to deny some obscure detail of the accusation, or to contradict each other on irrelevant points.

Vyshinsky: Was your directing centre organized on the basis of terrorism?

Smirnov: Yes, it was.

Vyshinsky: Were you a member of the centre?

Smirnov: Yes, I was.

Vyshinsky: Consequently, Trotsky's instructions were meant for you too?

Smirnov: Yes, they were communicated to me.

Vyshinsky: Did you accept them?

Smirnov: Yes, I did.

Vyshinsky: How then can you maintain that Trotsky was no authority for you?

Smirnov: I obeyed his instructions and communicated them to the centre. The centre accepted them, but I did not take part in their work.

Vyshinsky: Did that centre exist?
Smirnov: What sort of a centre?
Vyshinsky: Accused Mrachkovsky, did that centre exist?
Mrachkovsky: Yes, it did.
Vyshinsky: Accused Zinoviev, did the centre exist?
Zinoviev: Yes, it did.
Vyshinsky: Accused Yevdokimov, did the centre exist?
Yevdokimov: Yes.
Vyshinsky: Accused Bakayev, did that centre exist?
Bakayev: Yes, it did.
Vyshinsky: Smirnov, how then dare you maintain that it did not exist? Did you receive instructions from Trotsky?
Smirnov: Yes, I did.
Vyshinsky: Did those instructions contain direct references to the need for a terroristic struggle against the party leaders?
Smirnov: Quite true.
Vyshinsky: Against whom was that struggle to be directed in the first instance?
Smirnov: No names were mentioned.
Vyshinsky: But you understood that the terroristic attempts were to be directed against comrade Stalin, didn't you?
Smirnov: Yes, that is what I understood.
Vyshinsky: Did you communicate this to your colleagues?
Smirnov: Yes, I did.
Vyshinsky: And so did you or did you not have direct communications with Trotsky?
Smirnov: I had two addresses.
Vyshinsky: I am asking you whether there were any direct communications.
Smirnov: I had two addresses.
Vyshinsky: Answer, was there any communication?
Smirnov: If possessing addresses amounts to communication.
Vyshinsky: And what does it amount to?
Smirnov: I said that I had received two addresses.

Vyshinsky: Did you maintain personal communication with Trotsky?
Smirnov: There was no personal communication.
Vyshinsky: Was there communication with Trotsky by mail?
Smirnov: There was communication by mail with Trotsky's son.
Vyshinsky: The letter you received – was it sent to you by Trotsky's son or by Trotsky himself?
Smirnov: That was a letter from Trotsky himself.
Vyshinsky: That is all I have been asking.

Above: Trotsky, exiled in Norway, desperately tries to tune in to news bulletins from Radio Moscow during the nightmare summer of 1936.
Right: Leon Sedov.
Opposite page: May Day celebrations, Moscow, 1936. Front row, left to right, Gamarnik, Voroshilov, Budienny and Yagoda.
Top right, Stalin takes the salute

Did you then have any communication with Trotsky? Yes or no?

Smirnov: I said that I had written a letter to Trotsky, and had received a reply from him.

Vyshinsky: Was that communication or not?

Smirnov: Yes, it was.

Vyshinsky: Accused Valentin Olberg, you were connected with Trotsky through his son Sedov, were you not? As Trotsky's agent, and on Trotsky's direct instructions, you were sent to the U.S.S.R. Your task was to prepare and carry out an attempt on the life of comrade Stalin. Am I right?

Olberg: Yes, that is true.

Vyshinsky: And through your brother you were connected with the Gestapo, the German political police, were you not?

Olberg: Yes, that is also true.

Vyshinsky: Now tell us in what way you prepared this terrorist act?

Olberg: Even before my arrival in the U.S.S.R. I had learned from Trotsky's son that an underground Trotskyist organization existed in the U.S.S.R., with Smirnov and Mrachkovsky as its leaders. I knew that Bakayev was also a member. Here, in the U.S.S.R., I learned from a man called Fedotov that

terrorist groups had already been formed. All I had to do was to draw up a plan for the attempt on Stalin's life. This was to take place in Moscow on 1 May 1936.

That is to say, during the annual May Day celebrations which would be attended by immense crowds, including many foreign visitors.

Vyshinsky: And what prevented you from carrying out this plan?

Olberg: My arrest.

Vyshinsky: Did you send any progress reports to Trotsky's son.

Olberg: Yes, I did. I wrote to him repeatedly, and received a letter stating that our old friend insisted that I should submit my 'doctor's thesis' by 1 May.

Vyshinsky: 'Doctor's thesis'? What is that?

Olberg: That was the code term for the assassination of Stalin.

Vyshinsky: And the old friend – who was meant by that?

Olberg: The old friend was – Trotsky.

Two other defendants, Berman-Yurin and Fritz David, testified that they had taken their orders from Trotsky in

Copenhagen in November 1932.

Berman-Yurin: I arrived there one day towards the end of November. It was early in the morning. I was met at the station by a man called Grylevich, and we went to see Trotsky. Grylevich introduced me to him and then went away. I remained alone with Trotsky. We had two conversations. Trotsky told me that . . . Stalin must be physically destroyed, because all the other methods of attack had proved ineffective. For this purpose, he said, we needed courageous people, people ready to sacrifice themselves in order to perform this, as he put it, historic task. In addition to Stalin, Trotsky added, it was necessary to assassinate Kaganovich and Voroshilov. During our conversation Trotsky paced nervously up and down the room and spoke of Stalin with extraordinary hatred.

Vyshinsky: Did you agree to organize the attempt on Stalin's life?

Berman-Yurin: Yes, I did. Trotsky then told me to get ready for the journey to Moscow. The attempt on Stalin, he said, should, if possible, be staged at a plenary session of the Executive Committee; or, better still, at the Congress of the Communist International. The shot must ring out in a large assembly, so as to have tremendous repercussions far beyond the

Trotsky in exile in Turkey with his
daughter Zinaida. The two men behind
them were later exposed as GPU agents
who had infiltrated his circle.
Opposite page: an official portrait
of Vyshinsky in 1937

borders of the U.S.S.R., and so as to give rise to a mass movement all over the world. Trotsky said that I should avoid any contact with his sympathizers in Moscow. I replied that as I did not know anyone in Moscow, I would find it dif-

ficult to do anything. I was then told to get in touch, in Moscow, with Fritz David. This I did. David and I discussed our plan, and began our preparations. At first we thought that it would be possible to make the attempt on comrade Stalin's

life at the Thirteenth Plenary Session of the Executive of the Communist International. Fritz David was to secure an admission ticket for me; I was to fire the shot. But just before the session, it turned out that he could not obtain the ticket.

We postponed the attempt until the Congress of the Comintern, which was to have been convened in September 1934. I gave Fritz David a Browning pistol and some bullets. Just before the opening of the Congress, he informed me that he had once more failed to obtain a ticket for me. But, as he himself was to be present at the Congress, we agreed that he should carry out the attempt. Several days later I met him again; he said he would be unable to aim his pistol

Above and opposite page: Boris Efimov, the caricaturist, had flattered Trotsky when he was in power, but with the card trick played here entitled 'Terror' he illustrated the most abject accusations of the Stalinist Press at Stalin – that there would be too many other people in the box which he himself was to occupy.

Curiously, not one of these alleged terrorist plans was ever carried out, apart of course from the assassination of Kirov which, as Khrushchev now hints, Stalin himself may have planned. Nor did any of the defendants, in this and the following trials, produce any document or letter indicating that Trotsky had instructed anyone to engage in terrorist attempts; nor that any of them had ever been in contact with him since his banishment from Russia. Berman-Yurin and Fritz David claimed that Trotsky had received them in Copenhagen, at the Hotel Bristol. But it soon turned out that this hotel, once well known, had ceased to exist. It had been demolished years earlier. All this did not discourage Vyshinsky.

Vyshinsky: Comrade Judges, Members of the Military Tribunal of the Supreme Court: for days you have most carefully and attentively examined the depositions and the proofs that the prosecution has submitted to you. With the greatest possible care you have subjected to investigation and to judicial scrutiny every such piece of evidence – every act, every circumstance, every step taken by the defendants: by those defendants who for years have added crime to crime in their campaign against the Soviet state. Horrible and monstrous is the chain of their crimes against our socialist Fatherland – each of these crimes deserves the severest condemnation and the severest punishment. Horrible and monstrous is the guilt of these criminals and murderers who have raised their hands against the leaders of our party, against comrades Stalin, Voroshilov, Zhdanov, Kaganovich, Ordjonikidze, Kossior, Postyshev, against our leaders, the leaders of the Soviet state. Our people demands and expects from you a just, unfaltering and implacably stern decision concerning the fate of these people, these contemptible murderers, these vile and insolent enemies of the land of the Soviets. Under difficult conditions of class struggle we are building a new socialist society, a new Soviet state. Every step in our progress is

Right: Trotsky, his wife Natalya and their son Leon Sedov in exile — and in isolation.

Vyshinsky, the public prosecutor of the U.S.S.R.

THE MOSCOW TRIAL WAS FAIR
by
D. N. PRITT, K.C., M.P.
(reprinted by courtesy of the "News Chronicle")
27 August
with additional material
on the personalities and background
of the trial by PAT SLOAN
ONE PENNY

accompanied by desperate resistance on the part of our enemies, who are the filth and the scum of the old society. Comrade Stalin not only foretold the inevitable resistance of those elements hostile to the cause of socialism; he also predicted the possibility that Trotskyist counter-revolutionary groups might be revived. This trial has fully proved the great wisdom of his prophecy. The defendants have linked their fate with that of the fascists and the agents of foreign secret police departments. They have lost all scruples and have gone to the utmost limits of duplicity and deceit, of perfidy and of treachery. These capitalist mad dogs have tried to tear limb from limb the best of the best of our Soviet land. They have killed one who was most dear to us, an admirable and wonderful man, as bright and joyous as the smile of his lips was always bright and joyous, as our new life is bright and joyous – they have killed our Kirov. They have wounded us close to our very heart. They sought to sow confusion and consternation in our ranks. Yet our great Fatherland is joyously flourishing and growing. With great and peerless love the toilers of the whole world speak the name of Joseph Vissarionovich Stalin, the name of that great teacher and leader of the peoples of the U.S.S.R. From their gloomy underworld, Trotsky, Zinoviev and Kamenev have therefore sent this despicable call: thrust him aside, kill him! The clandestine machinery began to work. Knives were sharpened, revolvers loaded, bombs charged; false documents were fabricated; secret connections with the Gestapo were established; the plot-

ters took up their positions and finally they shot and killed. Counter-revolutionaries do not merely dream of terror; they do not merely devise plans and plots for their outrages; they do not merely prepare these foul crimes – they commit them, they shoot, they kill.

After ranting like this for many hours, Vyshinsky wound up:

Vyshinsky: The enemy is cunning. A cunning enemy must not be spared. Our whole people has risen to its feet since these ghastly crimes have become known. Our whole people is quivering with indignation; and I, as representative of the State Prosecution, am joining my anger, my indignant voice, to the thunderous voices of millions. I should like to conclude by reminding you, comrade judges, of those demands which the law makes in cases of the gravest crimes against the state: I take the liberty of reminding you that it is your duty, once you find that all sixteen of these people are guilty of crimes against the state – that it is your duty to apply to them in full measure those articles of the law which the prosecution has proffered against them. **I demand that the mad dogs be shot! Every one of them should be shot!**

Now the defendants were called upon to make their last plea.
Kamenev: Twice my life has been spared. But there is a limit to everything. There is a limit even to the magnanimity of the working class; that limit we have now

reached. I am asking myself: is it an accident that here beside me, and beside Zinoviev, Yevdokimov, Bakayev and Mrachkovsky, there sit emissaries of foreign secret police departments, people with false passports, people of doubtful antecedents but undoubted connections with the Gestapo. This is not an accident. We are sitting side by side with these agents of foreign secret police departments, because our weapons were the same, because our arms were linked even before our fates were linked, here in the dock. We have served fascism. We have organized counter-revolution against socialism. We have prepared and paved the way for the interventionists. Such is the path we have taken, and such is the pit of contemptible treachery into which we have fallen.
Zinoviev: I should like to repeat that I am fully and utterly guilty. I am guilty of having been the organizer, second only to Trotsky, of that bloc whose chosen task was the killing of Stalin and Voroshilov. I was the principal organizer of Kirov's assassination. The party saw where we were going, and warned us; Stalin warned us scores of times; but we did not heed these warnings. We entered into alliance with Trotsky. My defective Bolshevism thus became transformed into anti-Bolshevism, and through Trotskyism I arrived at fascism. Trotskyism is a variety of fascism and Zinovievism a variety of Trotskyism.
Smirnov: My mistake, which turned out to be a crime, was that I, Ivan Smirnov, resumed contact with Trotsky, accepted terrorist instructions from him and conveyed them to others. I call upon all my

Герой убийства и измены
Не забывает правил гигиены.
Фашистские палачики живут
По предписаниям науки.
Палач, окончив каждодневный труд,
Трусливо умывает руки.

А. ЖАРОВ

comrades to fight against Trotsky and Trotskyism. There is no other path for our country than that in which Stalin is leading us; and there is not, nor can there be, any leadership other than Stalin's, the leadership that history has given us.

Golzman: Here in the dock beside me, Golzman, sits a gang of murderers, fascist murderers. I do not ask for mercy.

On 24 August, early in the afternoon, the President of the Court pronounced all sixteen defendants guilty of all the crimes of which they were accused. All sixteen were sentenced to death and executed. The court also ordered that Trotsky and his son, Leon Sedov, if they ever appeared in the U.S.S.R., should be apprehended and tried by the Military Tribunal.

Trotsky was then living in Norway, whose Labour government had given him refuge; and he had just finished writing a book under the eloquent title of *The Revolution Betrayed*. When the trial began he had declared in an interview:

Trotsky: The accusations levelled in the Moscow trial against the defendants and myself are not only false – they represent the greatest frame-up in all history.

Trotsky undertook to prove this, and to refute in detail every one of Vyshinsky's charges. He felt it his duty to speak up not only for himself but for all the defendants. However, on 29 August, Yakubovich, the Soviet Ambassador in Oslo, delivered this formal note to the Norwegian government:

Yakubovich: L. D. Trotsky has been using Norway as the base for his conspiratorial and terrorist activity. The Supreme Court of the U.S.S.R. has recently established this beyond any doubt. The Soviet government wishes to state that the continued granting of asylum to Trotsky by the Norwegian government will impair friendly relations between the U.S.S.R. and Norway and will violate the rules governing international relations.

It was commonly believed in Oslo that Moscow had threatened to apply reprisals and to cut off trade with Norway; and that it was to avert this threat that the Norwegian government decided to intern Trotsky. This is what Professor Koht, Norway's Foreign Minister at the time, said about these events.

Koht: My colleagues in the government were afraid of Soviet economic reprisals,

although the Russians did not in fact say that they would apply them. I did not believe that they would resort to commercial boycott; and I held that in any case our trade with Russia, with herring as our main export, was not important enough for us to become alarmed. I was therefore against the proposal that we should intern Trotsky. But I was outvoted by my colleagues in the cabinet.

Trotsky was not only interned, but also forbidden to communicate with the outside world – or to answer the charges that Stalin and Vyshinsky levelled at him. During five crucial months, he was reduced to complete silence.

Vyshinsky: Why does not Trotsky answer our accusations? Evidently he has nothing to say in self-defence – else he would have spoken up long ago.

And how did world opinion react? The trial of the sixteen took place just after

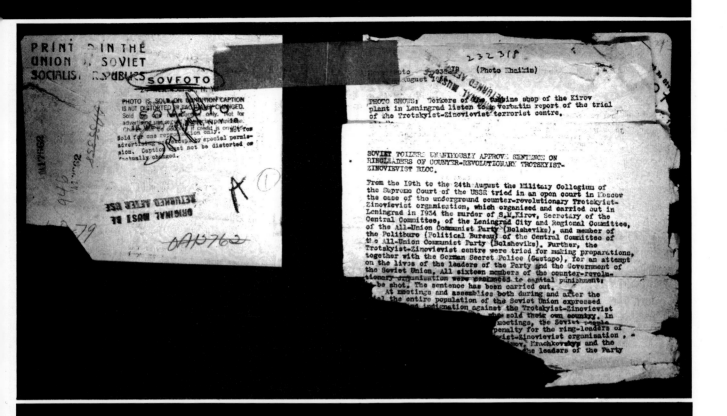

Hitler's armies had marched into the Rhineland and after Popular Front governments had been formed in France and Spain. The Labour movement and the leftist intelligentsia of the West looked to Stalin as their ally against Hitler. Consequently they were extremely wary of raising any protests against the Moscow purges. Might not Stalin retaliate by breaking up the Popular Fronts, withholding arms from the loyalist forces in Spain, and leaving Western Europe alone to face the Third Reich? And apart from all this, the sombre irrationality of the Moscow trials confused and confounded many. People who might have raised their voices against an infamy they were able to understand were utterly reluctant to protest against – and so to become involved in – a dark and bloody mystery. Stalin was acting on the Hitlerian principle that people usually disbelieve a small lie, but swallow a big one and the bigger the lie the better. The lie of the Moscow trials was so huge, so fantastic and so all-pervading that it was well-nigh unanswerable. It had the quality of something as immovable, as persistent and as powerful as reality itself. It had the reality of a nightmare. Surely, people wondered, Stalin could not have invented all the Trotskyist and Zinovievist crimes and conspiracies. And if he did

invent them, why do all the defendants admit their guilt? Few, very few, were those in the West who had any inkling of the techniques of interrogation used by the G.P.U., or of the whole background against which the trials were staged.

At this time the Stalinists exercised a strong influence on the intelligentsia in France, Spain, Britain and the United States; and upon these they brought to bear every kind of moral pressure, in order to prevent their lending the slightest support to any protest against the purges. Famous lawyers (among them a British K.C.), professors, authors, trade-union leaders and others vouched for Stalin's and Vyshinsky's integrity and justice. From Moscow, where the flower of Russian literature and art was being exterminated, the voices of Gorky, Sholokhov and Ehrenburg, the best-known Soviet writers, could be heard, as they joined in the chorus that filled the air with the cry: **'Shoot the mad dogs!'** Western literary celebrities like Theodore Dreiser, Leon Feuchtwanger, Henri Barbusse and Louis Aragon echoed the cry. Even a man like Romain Rolland, whom many regarded as the humanitarian conscience of his generation, defended Stalin's action. Bernard Shaw, who managed to admire both Trotsky and Stalin, expressed his perplexity in these words:

G. B. Shaw: I have spent nearly three hours in Stalin's presence and observed him with keen curiosity. And I find it just as hard to believe that he is a vulgar gangster as that Trotsky is an assassin.

The Trial of the Sixteen set the pattern for all the Moscow trials that were to follow. In January 1937 Pyatakov, Radek, Sokolnikov, Muralov, Serebriakov and others appeared in the dock. All these men, once eminent members of the Trotskyist opposition, had surrendered to Stalin and had made their recantations in 1927, 1928, 1929 and later. Pyatakov, Deputy Commissar of Heavy Industry, had been the moving spirit of Soviet industrialization; Radek was the 'Prince of Soviet Pamphleteers'; Sokolnikov, a former Soviet Chancellor of the Exchequer and Ambassador in London; Muralov, the ex-Inspector-General of the Soviet Armed Forces; and so on, and so on. The accusations piled up ever more incongruously and incredibly. Vyshinsky spoke of Trotsky's pact with Hitler and with the Emperor of Japan, a pact under which they were to assist him in his struggle against Stalin, while he, Trotsky, was working for the military defeat and dismemberment of the Soviet Union, and was organizing industrial sabotage; catastrophes in Soviet coal-

Among the accused at the second Moscow Trial ... Above left: Radek. Top: Sokolnikov. Centre: Muralov. Above: Pyatakov

mines and factories, and on railways; mass poisoning of Soviet workers; and, of course, attempts on the lives of Stalin and other Politbureau members.

Again the defendants echoed the Prosecutor and themselves elaborated the charges that he directed against them. Pyatakov, for instance, confessed that in December 1935 he had gone by plane from Berlin to Oslo, where he was to obtain instructions from Trotsky. The authorities of the Oslo airport, however, issued a statement declaring that no plane coming from Berlin had landed at the airport in December 1935, nor for many weeks before and after that date. Radek spoke of letters which Trotsky had written to him; but he did not pro-duce them – he said that he had burned them. This did not prevent his quoting, verbatim, long passages from those burned letters. The trial ended with the usual death sentences – only Radek and Sokolnikov were condemned to ten years' imprisonment each; but both were presently to die in prison.

Then came the Tukhachevsky trial. On 1 May 1937 Marshal Tukhachevsky, Deputy Commissar of Defence and the most able of the Red Army's commanders, stood beside Stalin on the Lenin Mausoleum in Moscow, reviewing the May Day parade. Eleven days later he was demoted, and the G.P.U. announced that he had been at the head of yet another Trotskyist conspiracy, in which his accomplices were Gamarnik, chief Political Commissar of the Soviet Armed Forces; General Yakir, Commander of the Leningrad Military District; General Uborevich, Commander of the Western Military District; General Kork, Commander of Moscow's Military Academy; General Primakov, Deputy Commander in Chief of the Cavalry, and others. Without any open trial, all these generals were condemned to death and executed. Four marshals, Voroshilov, Budienny, Blücher and Yegorov, signed the death sentence; of these four, Blücher and Yegorov themselves soon faced the firing squad. The purge in the armed forces affected twenty-five thousand officers, and decapitated the Red Army

Above: Red Square, May Day 1937. Taking the salute on Lenin's mausoleum, bottom row, left to right, Marshals Tukhachevsky, Belov, Voroshilov, Yegorev and Budienny; top row, left to right, Stalin, Kaganovich, Akulsov, Andreev, Dimitrov, Yezhov, Mikoyan, Molotov, Chubar and Kalinin.
Left: Tukhachevsky and his wife Nina.
Opposite page: Tukhachevsky

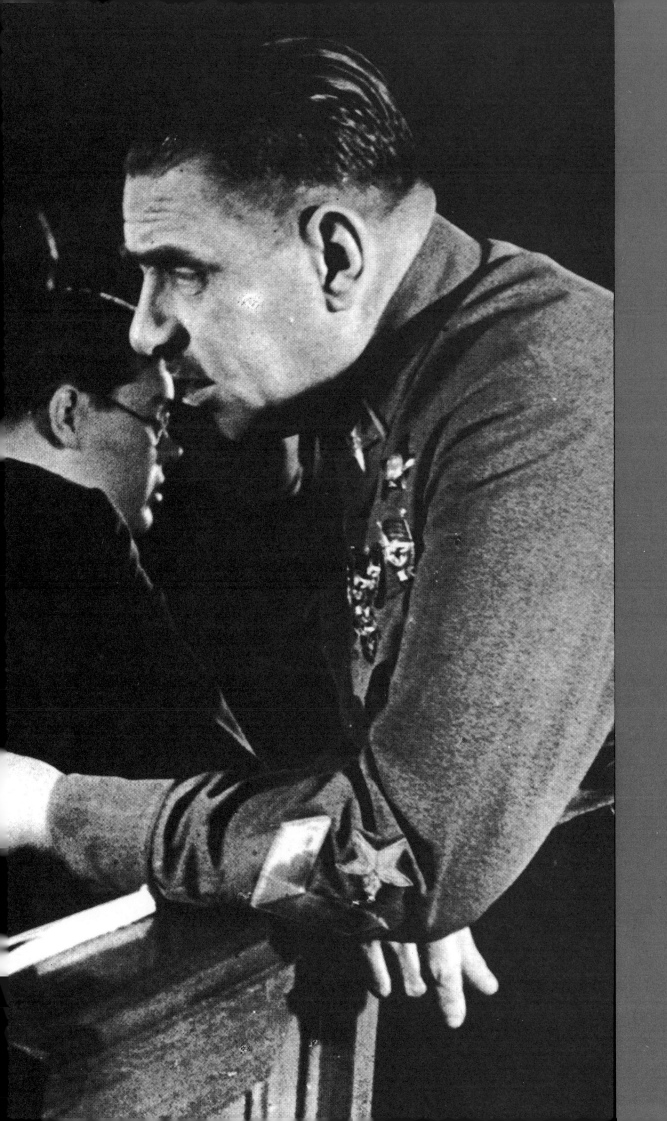

Marshals Gamarnik, Yegorov and Blucher at the Extraordinary Eighth All-Union Congress of Soviets in December, 1936

Propaganda photomontage, made in 1938 by Alexander Rodchenko, of Marshal Voroshilov, People's Commissar for Defence. Opposite page: General Kork, Commander of Moscow's Military Academy

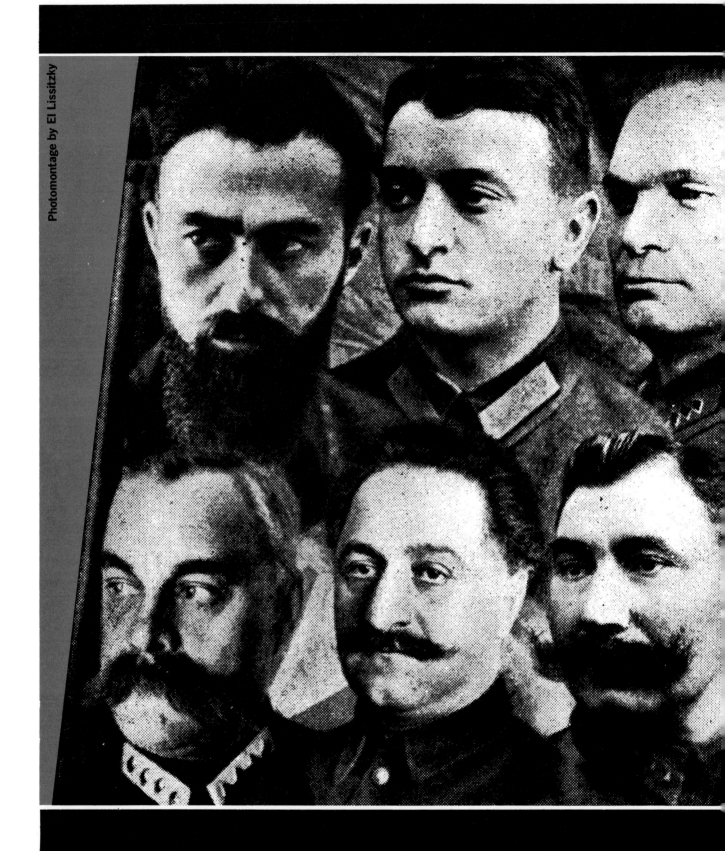

Above: Contemporary photomontage
of the Supreme Military Council
of the USSR. Top, left to right, Gamarnik,
Tukhachevsky, Yegorov,
Khalepsky, Orlov and Yakir.
Below, General Kamenev, Ordjonokidze,
Budienny, Alksnis, Muklevich, Eideman and
Uborevich. All were purged except
Budienny. Right: Stalin in conversation
with Voroshilov, 1936.
Far right: Budienny in conversation
with Vyshinsky, 1939

104

on the eve of the Second World War. Tukhachevsky and all his military colleagues have now been formally rehabilitated in the U.S.S.R., and declared completely innocent of the crimes that Stalin and Vyshinsky had imputed to them. Apart from this no light has yet been thrown upon the circumstances of the purge.

And so the terror spread, with appalling impetus; and the Soviet Union was as if trapped in a nightmare. No one was safe, not even the inquisitors or the hangmen. Yagoda, the head of the political police, was arrested; it was under Yezhov, his successor, that the delirium assumed its most horrible intensity – to this very day, the Russians speak with a shudder of the *Yezhovshchyna*, the days of Yezhov. Together with the G.P.U., all other Soviet secret services were purged. Those of their agents who worked outside the U.S.S.R. were lured back to Moscow to face accusations, and, ultimately, firing squads. One of these agents, Ignatz Reiss, Chief of the European network of the Soviet Counter-Intelligence, decided to resign from his post in protest. On 18 July 1937, he addressed from Paris the following message to the Central Committee in Moscow:

Reiss: I should have addressed this letter to you much earlier, on the day when, by order of the Father of the Peoples, Zinoviev and Kamenev were executed in the cellars of the Lubyanka prison. But I was silent then. I did not raise my voice in protest, For this I bear a grave responsibility. I shall try to mitigate my guilt . . . and thereby ease my conscience. I have marched with you so far, but I shall not go a step further. Our roads part. He who still remains silent becomes Stalin's accomplice – and a traitor to the working class and to socialism. I have struggled for socialism since I was twenty; and now, at forty, I have no wish to live by

Above: orphaned by Stalin — left to right, Roman Bernaut, son of Ignace Reiss; Nora and Vera Nin, daughters of the Spanish revolutionary Andres Nin; and Sieva Volkov, son of Trotsky's daughter Zinaida and of Platon Volkov, murdered by the GPU. Opposite page: Ignace Reiss

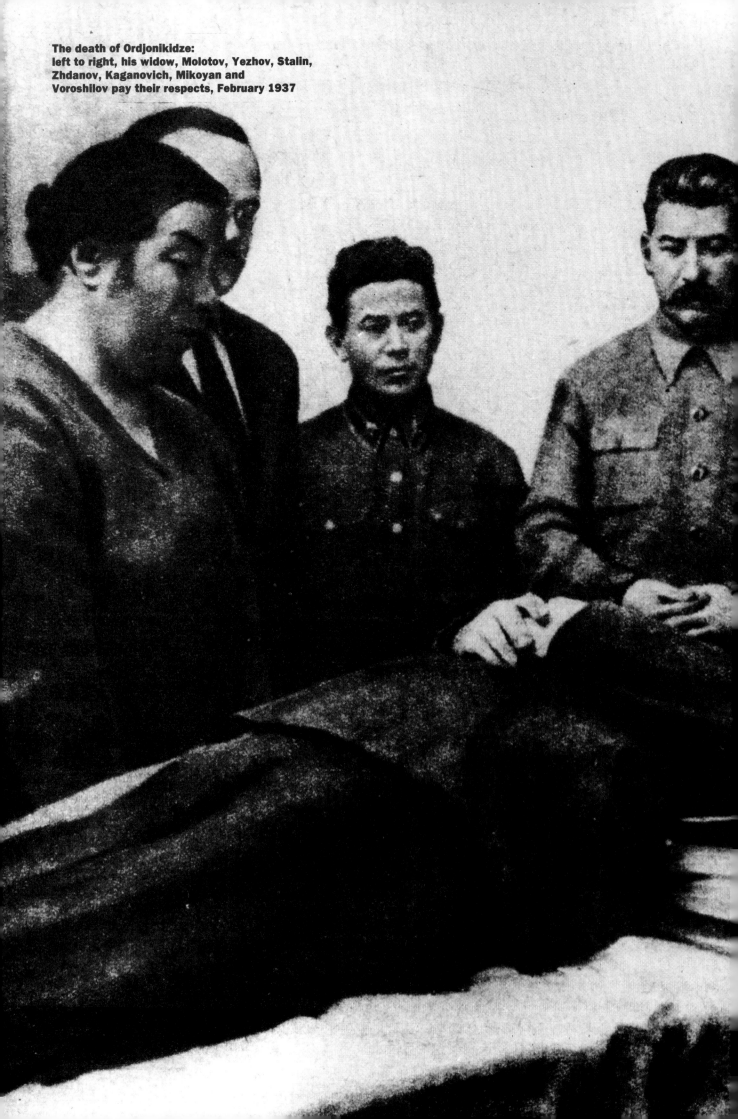

The death of Ordjonikidze:
left to right, his widow, Molotov, Yezhov, Stalin,
Zhdanov, Kaganovich, Mikoyan and
Voroshilov pay their respects, February 1937

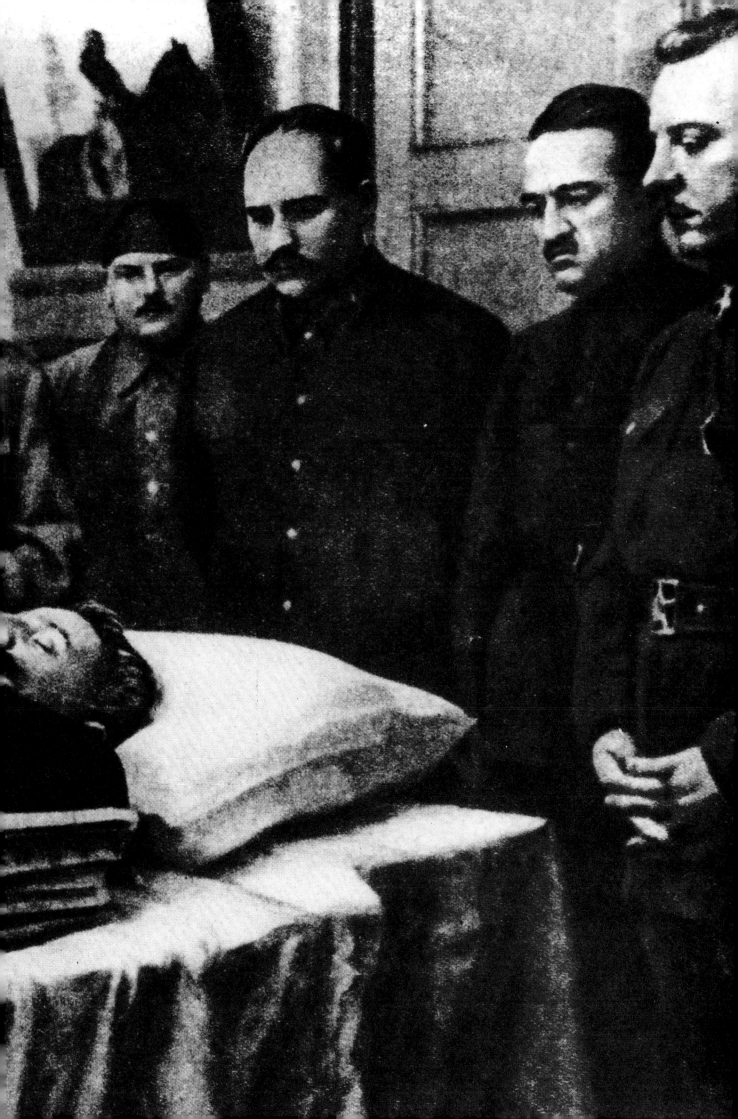

СТАЛЬНЫЕ ЕЖОВЫ РУКАВИЦЫ

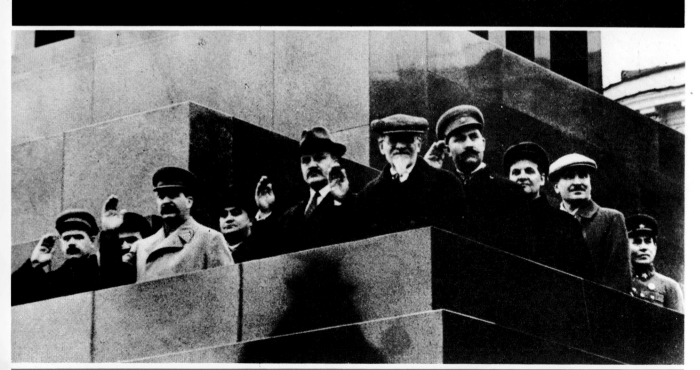

May Day 1938 in Moscow — Nikolai Yezhov on the extreme right, wearing GPU uniform.
Top: 'Yezhov's Steel Glove' — caricature by Boris Efimov, 1937.
Opposite page: Yezhov, an official portrait

Yezhov's grace . . . The day is not far off when international socialism will sit in judgement upon all the crimes committed in these last ten years. Nothing will be forgotten, nothing forgiven. The Leader of Genius, the Father of the Peoples, the Rising Sun of Socialism – will have to account for all his deeds. At the great and public trial that is coming, there will be many witnesses, alive and dead; all will speak; and this time all will tell the truth, the whole truth. All of them, those who have been innocently slandered and slaughtered, they will all come back to the witness box – and the international labour movement will rehabilitate them all, the Kamenevs and Mrachkovskys, the Smirnovs and Muralovs . . . all those alleged spies, saboteurs and Gestapo agents. No, I cannot march with you any further. I am going back to Lenin's teachings and to Lenin's cause. I am sending back to you the Order of the Red Banner which you awarded me in 1928. To wear it now, when so many hangmen are wearing it, would be beneath my dignity . . .

Six weeks after he had written this letter Reiss was found dead, his body bullet-riddled on a road near Lausanne. The Swiss and French police had no doubt that he had died a victim of the G.P.U. Victor Krivitsky, another member of the Soviet Secret Service who then broke with Stalin, was to be found dead in a hotel in Washington a few years later . . . In February 1938 Leon Sedov, Trotsky's son, who figures in the Moscow trials as his father's chief assistant, died mysteriously in a Russian clinic in Paris. The G.P.U. terror raged in Spain during the civil war; its victims were members of the P.O.U.M., a semi-Trotskyist party, and Anarcho-Syndicalists – George Orwell has given us a glimpse of that terror in *Homage to Catalonia*. Andres Nin, the leader of the P.O.U.M., was kidnapped and assassinated; and there was no end to the witch-hunts and murders that demoralized the Republican parties even before Franco defeated them.
In March 1938 the last of the great Moscow trials took place, the trial of Rykov, Bukharin, Krestinsky, Rakovsky, Yagoda and seventeen other defendants. Rykov, we remember, had succeeded Lenin as the Soviet Prime Minister and had held that post for six years. Bukharin had been the chief Bolshevik theoretician and head of the Communist Inter-

national. Rakovsky had been Premier of the Soviet Government of the Ukraine and later Ambassador in London and Paris. Krestinsky had been Secretary of the Central Committee, Commissar of Finance and Ambassador in Berlin. Yagoda – need it be recalled? – had been the chief of the G.P.U.
At the opening of the trial Krestinsky refused to make the confession expected of him. Vyshinsky fumed, and after a day's proceedings Krestinsky was led back to his cell unbroken. What happened to him during the night that followed we do not know. But the next day it was as a crushed man that he came back to the dock. He acted his prescribed part as if in a trance, confessing that he had met Trotsky and his son repeatedly in Berlin and elsewhere in Europe, had conspired with them, and brought them in contact with General von Seeckt, the Chief of the Reichswehr. Seeckt had paid out two million Goldmarks, nearly a million dollars, and other sums, to finance the conspiracy. Krestinsky depicted Trotsky, himself and the other defendants as agents not only of Hitler and the Mikado, but also of British Military Intelligence. In addition to having organized attempts on the lives of Stalin, Voroshilov, Kaganovich and Molotov, and to have caused railway catastrophes, colliery explosions and mass poisoning of workers, the defendants (so the prosecution stated) were also responsible for the murder of Maxim Gorky, the famous writer. And they had attempted to assassinate Lenin as early as 1918! Yagoda, who had for ten years been in charge of the persecution of the Trotskyists, now claimed to have been all this time merely a tool in Trotsky's hands. Alongside party leaders, commissars and ambassadors, there sat in the dock a group of distinguished medical men. One of them, Doctor Levin, a septuagenarian, had been Lenin's and Stalin's personal physician since the revolution; he was now charged with having poisoned Gorky at Yagoda's command. For many hours, in the course of several sessions, the doctors related how they had plied their poisonous trade within the walls of the Kremlin; and they described all manner of sadistic exploits in which they had allegedly indulged. Again the trial ended with death sentences and executions.
The trial of Bukharin and Rykov was the last of the monster trials; but this was not yet the end of the purges. There were

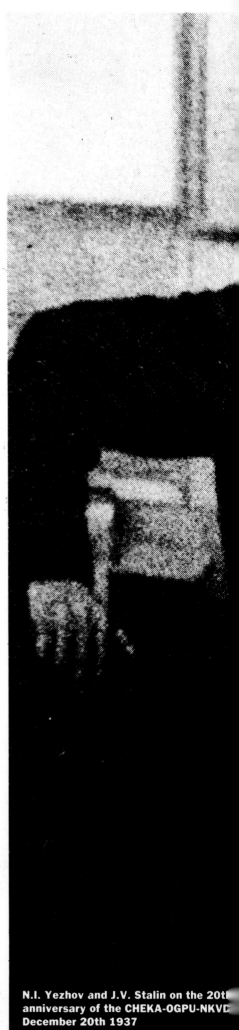

Nikolai Krestinsky

Above: 'Vaterland' — caricature by
Boris Efimov published in Izvestia on
March 5th 1938, showing, left to right,
Rykov, Chernov, Bukharin, Radek and
Trotsky dining courtesy of the Gestapo.
Opposite page: Christian Rakovsky

Above: Nikolai Bukharin shortly before his arrest.
Top: caricature by Boris Efimov (Izvestia, March 10th 1938)
showing Bukharin as Goebbels and Yagoda
as a Nazi butcher. The title of the book held by Bukharin is
'The Theory of Spying, Treachery and Terror'.
Left: Genrikh Yagoda

countless trials in which the defendants refused to confess, and which were therefore held in secret. And throughout the Yezhov period a terrible massacre went on in the concentration camps of the sub-Polar regions and of Siberia, where all the adherents of all the opposition groups, and even their relatives, were being systematically exterminated. This is how an eyewitness, an ex-inmate of the ill-famed Vorkuta camps in the Far North, describes the last acts of resistance of the oppositionists and their extermination (this account, signed only with the initials M.B., appeared in *Sotsialisticheskii Vestnik*, a Russian émigré Menshevik periodical):

Eyewitness: In my camp alone there were about a thousand old Trotskyists, who called themselves Bolshevik–Leninists; and about five hundred of these worked at the Vorkuta colliery. In the camps of the Pechora province there was a total of several thousand so-called orthodox Trotskyists, who had been in deportation since the year 1927 and who had still remained true to their political ideals and leaders. About this time – 1936–7 – apart from these genuine Trotskyists – there were more than a hundred thousand inmates of the camps in Vorkuta and elsewhere who, as party members or Komsomoltsy, had joined the Trotskyist opposition and had then at various times and for various reasons . . . been forced to recant, to admit their mistakes, and to leave the ranks of the opposition. All the same, the Trotskyists proper were the most numerous group. They arrived at the colliery in the summer of 1936 and were put up in two large shanties. They refused categorically to work in the pits. They worked only at the pitheads and for not more than eight hours a day, not ten or twelve hours as the regulations required and as all other inmates were compelled to do. They ignored camp regulations ostentatiously and in an organized manner. Most of them had spent about ten years in isolation, first in gaols, then in camps on the Solovky Islands and finally at Vorkuta. The Trotskyists were the only political prisoners who openly criticized the Stalinist 'general line' and openly and in an organized manner resisted the gaolers.

In the autumn of 1936, after the trial of Zinoviev and Kamenev, these oppositionists arranged camp meetings and demonstrations in honour of the executed comrades and leaders. Shortly thereafter they began a hunger strike – it began on 27 October 1936 and lasted one hundred and thirty-two days. The strikers protested against being transferred from previous places of deportation and penalized without open trial.

They demanded an eight-hour working day, the same food for all inmates, separation of political and criminal prisoners and the removal of invalids, women and old people from sub-Polar regions to areas with a milder climate. The decision to start the hunger strike was taken in open meeting. Sick and elderly prisoners were exempted, but they categorically rejected the exemption. So impressive was this act of protest and so complete was the solidarity of all participants that in March 1937, on orders from Moscow, the camp administration yielded on all points; and the strike came to an end.

But this was the deportees' last, and rather short-lived, success. Presently the terror came back with fresh fury. The food ration in the concentration camp was drastically reduced. The G.P.U. armed criminal prisoners with clubs and incited them against the oppositionists. There were indiscriminate shootings; and all political prisoners were isolated in a camp within the camp, surrounded by barbed wire and guarded day and night by a hundred heavily armed soldiers. And this, according to our eyewitness, is what happened next:

Eyewitness: One morning, towards the end of March 1938, twenty-five men, mostly prominent Trotskyists, were called out, given a kilogram of bread each and ordered to collect their belongings and prepare for a march. After a warm leavetaking from their friends, they left the shanties; there was a roll-call, and they were marched out. In about fifteen or twenty minutes a volley was suddenly fired about half a kilometre from the shanties, near the steep bank of a little river called the Upper Vorkuta. Then a few disorderly shots were heard, and silence fell. Soon the men of the escort came back and they passed by the shanties. Everyone understood upon what march the twenty-five had been sent.

On the next day no fewer than forty people were called out in this way, given their bread ration and ordered to get ready.

Eyewitness: Some were so exhausted that they could not walk; they were promised that they would be put on carts. With bated breath the people in the shanties listened to the creaking of the snow under the feet of those who were marched away. All sounds had already died down; yet everyone was still listening tensely. After about an hour, shots resounded across the tundra. The crowd in the shanties knew now what awaited them; but after the long hunger strike of the previous year, and many more months of freezing and starvation, they had not the strength to resist. Throughout April and part of May the executions in the tundra went on. Every day, or every other day, thirty or forty people would be called out . . . Communiqués were broadcast over the camp loudspeakers: 'For counter-revolutionary agitation, sabotage, banditry, refusal to work and attempts to escape, the following have been executed . . .' Once a large group of about a hundred people was taken out. As they marched away, they sang the Internationale; hundreds of voices in the shanties joined in the singing. In this way even the families of the oppositionists were executed – the wife of one of the Trotskyists walked on her crutches to the execution place. Children were left alive only if they were less than twelve years old. The massacre went on in all the camps of the Pechora province and lasted until May. At Vorkuta only a little over a hundred people were left alive in the huts. About two weeks passed away quietly. Then the survivors were sent back to the colliery, where they were told that Yezhov had been dismissed and that Beria was in charge of the G.P.U.

This is how the effect of this massacre and of the purges is described in *The Prophet Outcast*: 'While the trials in Moscow were engaging the world's awe-struck attention, the great massacre in the concentration camps passed almost unnoticed. It was carried out in such deep secrecy that it took years for the truth to leak out. The terror of the Yezhov period amounted to political genocide; it destroyed the whole species of the anti-Stalinist Bolsheviks.' During the remaining fifteen years of Stalin's rule no group was left in Soviet society, not even in the prisons and camps, that was capable of challenging him. No centre of independent political thinking had been allowed to survive. A tremendous gap had been torn in the nation's consciousness; its collective memory was shattered; the continuity of its revolutionary traditions was broken; and its capacity to form and crystallize any nonconformist notions was destroyed. The Soviet Union was finally left, not merely in its practical politics, but even in its hidden mental processes, with no alternative to Stalinism. Trotsky, having left Norway, unceasingly and untiringly denounced the purges and the terror; but even he was not fully aware that all anti-Stalinist forces in the Soviet Union had been wiped out; that Trotskyism, Zinovievism and Bukharinism had all drowned in blood and had, like some Atlantis, vanished from all political horizons.

The photographs on this and the following seven pages are taken from a Soviet album published in Moscow in 1934 celebrating the construction of the Belomor-Baltic Canal. Since the work was carried out by tens of thousands of political prisoners — so-called 'enemies of the State' — who were brought from concentration camps all over the Soviet Union and guarded by officers of the OGPU, the pictures unwittingly provide a unique record of the Soviet labour camp system. Above: The original Soviet caption to this photograph of one of the guards in the camp reads: 'Guns are held like this, not to frighten anyone, but just out of convenience'.
Opposite page: Breaking rocks to build a sluice.

Above: 'Labour will
re-educate them'.
Right: 'Reforging',
the camp's newspaper.
Opposite page: top,
'Long live the leadership
of the OGPU';
below, from the right,
Khrushchev, Kaganovich
and Yagoda on site

Не подлежит распр. за пределы лагерей

ПЕРЕКОВКА

НА ФРОНТЕ СТРОИТЕЛЬСТВА 7 БОЕУЧАСТКА

ПРОИЗВОДСТВЕННЫЙ
БЮЛЛЕТЕНЬ
7 боевого участка
БЕЛБАЛТЛАГ ОГПУ
ВЫХОДИТ ЕЖЕДНЕВНО
ОРГАН КВЧ
15 мая 1933 г. № 72

ПОРА КОНЧАТЬ
РАБОТЫ!
С этим железным
решением выходите
на канал и добирай-
те остатки скалы и
грунтов вчистую!
(Из приказа за № 39).

Каждый день затяжки работ позорит честь ударников
Краснознаменного севера.

Все, как один, от прораба до землекопа — на штурм,
чтобы 17-го мая рапортовать: Сосновец и Шижня

Above: 'Thousands of people take a shovel
in their hands for the first time'.
Below: 'The transference of the Murmanka River,
by prisoner-painter Krasilnikov'

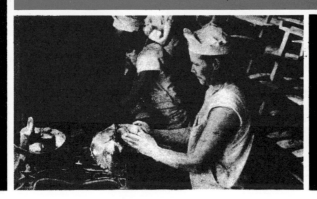

Above: 'Kazhak
shockworker with the
banner of his brigade'.
Left: The camp's bakery.
Opposite page: top,
'Move a rock, make way
for a sluice';
centre, 'We will teach
Mother Nature a lesson,
that's how we acquire our
freedom';
bottom, the exit of the
canal into the White Sea

"Not Guilty!"

In the spring of the year 1938 the public acts of the Great Purges, the series of the great Moscow trials, came to an end. The trial of Bukharin and his comrades was the last of the series. A year later, in March 1939, at the Eighteenth Party Congress, Stalin discoursed about the purges with triumphant mockery.

Stalin: The feature that distinguishes Soviet society today from any capitalist society is that our society contains no class antagonisms: the exploiting classes have been eliminated and the workers, peasants and intellectuals live and work in friendly collaboration. This community of interests forms the basis of our moral and political unity, the basis of the stability of the Soviet system. Some foreign journalists have been talking rubbish; they have said that by purging Soviet institutions of spies, assassins and wreckers like Trotsky, Zinoviev, Kamenev, Tukhachevsky, Bukharin and others, we have shaken the Soviet system and caused demoralization. One can only laugh at such cheap drivel. That Trotskyite–Bukharinite bunch of spies, assassins and wreckers – who needs that miserable band of venal slaves? Of what value could they be to our people? And who could be demoralized? In 1937 Tukhachevsky, Yakir, Uborevich and other fiends were sentenced to be shot. After that, the elections to the Supreme Soviet of the U.S.S.R. were held. In those elections 98·6 per cent of the total vote was cast for the Soviet government. At the beginning of 1938 Bukharin, Rykov and other fiends were sentenced to be shot. After that, the elections to the Supreme Soviet of the Union of the Republics were held. In those elections 99·4 per cent of the total vote was cast for the

Soviet government. Where are the symptoms of demoralization, we would like to know. And why was this demoralization not reflected in the results of the elections? To listen to those foreign drivellers one would think that if only the spies, assassins and wreckers had been left at liberty to wreak murder and to go on spying, then our Soviet institutions would have been far sounder and stronger. (LAUGHTER IN THE HALL.) Are not these gentlemen giving themselves away by defending so insolently the cause of spies, assassins and wreckers?

Yet Stalin also gave the Congress this promise:

Stalin: Comrades, we shall have no further need of resorting to mass purges.

Did he intend to keep this promise? The monster trials and the mass purges of the Yezhov period had indeed been left behind. It was now only a few months before the outbreak of the Second World War, and Stalin was anxious to restore Soviet morale. Yet, having exterminated the Trotskyists, Zinovievists

and Bukharinists, he still pressed on with one relentless purge, of which the world knew almost nothing – the strangest of all the purges, the secret purge of his own followers, the Stalinists. It was Khrushchev who first revealed the scale of that purge. In the 'secret speech' at the Twentieth Congress, in February 1956, he disclosed that Stalin had branded as enemies of the people, and sent to their death, no fewer than 70 per cent of all the members of the Stalinist Central Committee elected at the Seventeenth Party Congress in 1934. Stalin had similarly ordered the execution of most of the delegates to that Congress, that is over 1,100 delegates, nearly all of them Stalinists.

The Seventeenth Congress, it should be remembered, was officially labelled the Congress of Victors, because at it Stalin and his adherents celebrated their triumph over all the oppositions.

Yet as the Great Purges proceeded, even some of Stalin's most devoted and fanatical followers grew uneasy, expressed doubts, sought to mitigate the terror, even to limit Stalin's power. Inevitably the terror hit them too. Many members of the Politbureau and the Central Committee, several Vice-Premiers and many Ministers, branded 'enemies of the people', were executed either after secret trials or without any trial whatsoever. Rudzutak, chief of the trade unions, Mezhlauk, Chairman of the State Planning Commission, Rukhimovich, Chief of the Supreme Council of the National Economy, Postyshev and Kossior, Politbureau members and Khrushchev's predecessors as party bosses of the Ukraine; Eikhe, party boss of Siberia; these and many, many others perished in this way. These men were

Above right: caricature by Boris Efimov showing Bukharin and Trotsky as a double-headed 'mad dog of Fascism'. Opposite page: Stalin in 1939

completely taken aback and utterly crushed by the unexpected accusations – there was no limit to their gloom and despair. Here, for instance, are extracts from letters which Eikhe addressed to Stalin from the dungeon in which he spent the last two years of his life:

Eikhe: There is, believe me, no misery more bitter than to sit in the gaol of a government for which I have always fought. The investigation of my case has been concluded, and I have been given access to the documents. Had I been guilty of even one-hundredth of the crimes with which I am now being charged, I would not have dared to address you thus before my execution. But I am not guilty of a single one of the crimes laid against me. Never have I told you a word of falsehood; nor am I lying to you now, as I stand with both feet in the grave. My whole case, dear Joseph Vissarionovich, is a typical example of provocation, slander and violation of elementary justice.

Eikhe had been one of the dozen or so men who ruled Russia in the early and middle thirties – he had belonged to Stalin's closest entourage – and he had zealously helped to support Stalin against all rivals, critics and opponents. Hence the intimate personal tone of his appeals to Stalin.

Eikhe: I shall now touch upon the one really disgraceful act of my life . . . my confession, in which I admitted to counter-revolutionary activity. It was in making this confession that I truly rendered myself guilty, gravely guilty, against the party and against yourself. But this is what happened: I was unable to endure the tortures to which Ushakov and Nikolayev subjected me, especially Ushakov. He tortured me even while my broken ribs were causing me agony; in this way he forced me to accuse myself and others. He dictated to me most of my confession. Whenever any part of the tale that he fabricated did not properly hang together, I was forced to sign another variant of the story. The same thing was done to Rukhimovich and Mezhlauk. I implore you, re-examine my case – not in order to spare me, but in order to unmask the vile provocation.

There was no answer from Stalin's office. Eikhe was brought before a secret court, and there he made his last plea:

Eikhe: In none of these so-called confessions is there a single syllable that comes from me with the exception of the signature. From the moment of my arrest, the examining magistrate tortured me. The most important thing for me is that I can tell the court, the party and Stalin, that I am not guilty. I will die believing in the truth embodied in our party policy.

What was most terrifying in this holocaust was the utter helplessness of its victims. Not a single voice of protest, not a single lament or cry of despair, managed to pierce the walls of the prison or to break through the national chorus of adulation for Stalin.

The only voice of protest that the world heard in those years was the voice of Leon Trotsky, who had been exiled from the U.S.S.R.

Even Trotsky was not always able to protest. The first of the Moscow trials,

Above right: Eikhe (front, second from left) in happier days at Tiflis in 1934 with Kirov (extreme left), Stalin and Ordjonikidze (extreme right). Right: left to right, Mezhlauk, Rudzhutak, Khrushchev and Andreev. Opposite page: R.I. Eikhe

Top: Stalin posing with members of the
Politburo and actors of the Moscow
Theatre in 1938. Yezhov is shown fifth
from the right in the top row.
Above: in the same photograph,
published in 1949 to celebrate Stalin's
70th birthday, Yezhov has
been obliterated by the retouchers.

2c

TRU

ABOUT THE MO

No. 1   NEW

TROTSKY
MOSCO

John Dewey Hea

Noted Publicists Hear Trotsky; Stalinists Fear To Face Issue

H

A preliminary Commission of Inquiry headed by Dr. John Dewey, America's foremost liberal educator and philosopher, began this week in Mexico to take the testimony of Leon Trotsky as the first phase of the work of an international commission of inquiry into the Moscow trial.

The demand for an impartial commission of in ed in this country and abroad by great labor

Published by
PIONEER PUBLISHERS
100 Fifth Ave.,   New York
Bundle orders $1 per 100,
Send checks or money
order with orders.

Editor: MAX SHACHTMAN

JTH

COW TRIALS

, N. Y.   401   APRIL, 1937

BARES
W FRAUD

s Mexico Inquiry

OES NOT CONFESS!

ONLY TRUTH CAN UNMASK FRAME - UP

These pages seek
truth about th
the most
h

139

the trial of Zinoviev and Kamenev, found him in Norway. The socialist government had received him there with honours and given him refuge. But the same government, intimidated by Stalin's threats, then interned Trotsky, kept him in hermetic isolation, and for many months prevented his answering Stalin's charges. Only after he had found a new refuge in Mexico could Trotsky speak up. He organized a so-called counter-trial. In vain did he seek to associate with the counter-trial any of the communist or socialist parties, groups or any trade unions, or, indeed, any liberal or radical organizations. Few, very few, were those in the West who were prepared to defend Stalin's victims or to treat the Moscow trials as frame-ups. The counter-trial was therefore conducted by a small and not very influential body of men, who formed a special commission of inquiry. Presiding over the Commission was John Dewey, the American philosopher and educationist, the only member of the Commission who spoke with recognized moral authority.

The most important part of the counter-trial consisted in the Commission's cross-examination of Trotsky himself. As the American government would not allow Trotsky entry into the United States, the cross-examination took place in Mexico City at the home of Diego Rivera, the famous painter, with whom Trotsky was staying at the time. Here is a description of the scene, by several eyewitnesses:

Eyewitness 1: The atmosphere was tense. There was a police guard outside. Visitors were searched for guns and identified by one of Trotsky's secretaries who was himself armed. The French windows facing the street were covered – behind each window there was a barricade of sandbags and brick.

Eyewitness 2: These barricades had been completed the night before.

Eyewitness 3: About fifty people were present during the hearings, among them photographers and reporters.

Eyewitness 1: The hearings were conducted as in an American court. Dewey had invited the Soviet Embassy, and the Communist Parties of the United States and of Mexico, to send their representatives and take part in the cross-examination. His invitations were ignored or rejected.

Dewey opened the hearings:

Dewey: This Commission is neither a court nor a jury. We are here neither to defend nor to prosecute Leon Trotsky. We are not here to pronounce a verdict. We are an investigating body. Our function is to hear whatever testimony Mr Trotsky may present to us, to cross-examine him and to give the results of our investigation to the full Commission. The Commission of Inquiry was initiated by the American Committee for the Defense of Leon Trotsky. In the United States it has long been customary for public-spirited citizens to organize committees for the purpose of securing fair trials in cases where there was suspicion concerning the impartiality of the court. Such were the Tom Mooney Defense Committee and the Sacco–Vanzetti Defense Committee. Membership of such committees does not imply anything more than the belief that the accused is entitled to a fair trial. Twice in their absence both Leon Trotsky and his son Leon Sedov have been declared guilty by the highest tribunal of the Soviet Union. And Trotsky's repeated questions and demands have been ignored. Therefore it became part of the function of this defence committee to initiate the formation of an impartial body before which

his side of the case could be heard. The conscience of the world is not as yet satisfied on this historic issue. This world conscience demands that Mr Trotsky be not finally condemned before he has had full opportunity to present whatever evidence is in his possession. If Leon Trotsky is guilty of the acts with which he is charged, no condemnation can be too severe. That he has been condemned without the opportunity to be heard is a matter of utmost concern.

Trotsky's examination began on 10 April 1937, lasted a full week and took up thirteen long sessions. It was so detailed that it is hardly possible to summarize it here. But shortly before the hearings, Trotsky himself gave the gist of his case in a speech he intended to transmit in English to a meeting in New York. Here are the most striking passages of that speech:

Trotsky: Dear Listeners, Comrades and Friends! The theme of my address is the Moscow trial. I will appeal not to your passions, not to your nerves, but to reason. I do not doubt that reason will be found on the side of truth. Moscow resorts to all kinds of measures to force me, the principal accused, to keep silent. Yielding to Moscow's terrible economic pressure, the Norwegian government placed me under lock and key. How lucky it is that the magnanimous hospitality of Mexico has permitted us, my wife and I, to face the new trial, not under imprisonment but in freedom! But all the wheels have again been set in motion to force me once more into silence. Why does Moscow so fear the voice of a single man? Only because I know the truth, the whole truth. Only because I have nothing to hide. Only because I am ready to appear before a public and impartial committee of inquiry, with documents, facts and testimonies in my hands, and to disclose the last detail of the truth. I declare: if this Commission decides that I am

Above: Trotsky shaking hands with Dr John Dewey.
Opposite page: Trotsky in Mexico, 1938. Behind him, left to right, Diego Rivera, Natalya Sedova Trotsky, Riba Hansen (an American Trotskyist), Andre Breton, Frida Kahlo Rivera, Jean van Heijenoort (Trotsky's secretary)

Below: Trotsky in Mexico, February 26th 1938,
refuting the accusations
levelled against him at the Moscow Trials.
Opposite page: the tragedy of exile —
Trotsky, his grandson Sieva Volkov, his old friends
from the days of the revolution
Alfred and Marguerite Rosmer, his wife Natalya

guilty in the slightest degree of the crimes which Stalin imputes to me, I pledge in advance to place myself voluntarily in the hands of the executioners of the G.P.U. That, I hope, is clear. Have you all heard? I make this declaration before the entire world. I ask the press to publish my words in the farthest corners of our planet. But if the Commission establishes – do you hear me? – if the Commission establishes that the Moscow trials are a conscious and premeditated frame-up, constructed with the bones and nerves of human beings, I will not ask my accusers to place themselves voluntarily before a firing squad. No, the eternal disgrace in the memory of human generations will be sufficient for them!

Do the accusers in the Kremlin hear me? I throw my defiance in their faces. And I await their reply. The trial of Zinoviev and Kamenev centred upon the charge of terrorism. The trial of Pyatakov and Radek centres no longer on terror, but on the alliance of the Trotskyists with Nazi Germany and Japan . . . Radek and Pyatakov have confessed to frightful crimes. But those crimes do not make sense from the point of view of the defendants. With the aid of terror, sabotage and an alliance with the imperialists (so we are told) Radek and Pyatakov aimed to re-establish capitalism in the Soviet Union. Why? Throughout their entire lives they struggled against capitalism. Perhaps they were guided by personal motives:

the lust for power? The thirst for gain? But under no regime would Pyatakov and Radek occupy higher positions than those they occupied before their arrest.

Radek had been, even under Stalin, the most celebrated Soviet journalist. Pyatakov had been the chief manager of Soviet industry.

Trotsky: Only an opposition composed of cretins could think that an alliance with Hitler and the Mikado, both of whom are doomed to defeat in the next war, that such an absurd, inconceivable and senseless alliance with doomed rulers could afford to the opposition anything but disgrace and ruin. On the

We are proud i my dear... ... to
have you in our ranks... ... will
ful example of... ... devotion for our... ... bravery
you with... ...
Live long... ...
Long may... ...
fraternally
Leon Trotzky
24 / V
...

other hand, such an alliance – of the Trotskyists with Hitler – is indispensable for Stalin. The G.P.U. says: 'If the alliance does not exist, it is necessary to fabricate it.' Normal people, following the dictates of their own free will, would never have been able to conduct themselves as did Zinoviev, Kamenev, Radek, Pyatakov and the other men in the dock. Devotion to ideas, political dignity, the simple instinct of self-preservation, would have forced them to struggle for themselves, for their personalities, for their interests, for their lives. The only reasonable and fitting question is this: who brought these people to such a state that all their human reflexes were destroyed? And how did he do it? There is a very simple principle in jurisprudence, one which holds the key to many secrets: *is fecit cui prodest*; he who benefits by it is the culprit. The entire conduct of the men in the dock has been dictated from beginning to end not by their own ideas and interests, but by the interests of the ruling clique. And the pseudo-plot, the confessions, the theatrically unreal court proceedings and the entirely real executions, all were arranged by one and the same hand. Whose hand? *Cui prodest?* Who benefits? The hand of Stalin! All the rest is deceit, falsehood and idle babbling. In the trials there figured no fighters, no conspirators, but only puppets in the hands of the G.P.U. They played assigned roles. The aim of the disgraceful performance? To eliminate the whole opposition; to poison the very source of critical thought, to confirm Stalin's totalitarian regime.

Trotsky produced the facts and the testimonies which established his own alibi and by implication the alibis of the Moscow trial victims – facts and testimonies which proved, for instance, that Payatokov and the other defendants could not have had with Trotsky any of those meetings upon which they dwelt in their confessions. Trotsky laid before the Commission of Inquiry his enormous archives and all his correspondence.

Trotsky: The examination of my correspondence, it seems to me, is of decisive importance for the determination of the political and moral personalities not only of myself but also of my correspondents. Vyshinsky has not been able to present to the Moscow Tribunal a single letter from myself, or a single document belonging to me. I am presenting thousands of letters. I ask no one to take me on trust. I am presenting facts and documents. I demand their verification. Among you, dear listeners, there must be not a few who say: 'The confessions of the accused are false, that is clear; but how was Stalin able to obtain such confessions; therein lies the secret!' In reality the secret is not so profound. The Inquisition, with a much more simple technique, extorted all sorts of confessions from its victims. The whole political atmosphere of the Soviet Union is impregnated with the spirit of the Inquisition. Perhaps in this world there are many heroes capable of bearing all kinds of torture, physical and moral, inflicted upon themselves and upon their wives and children. I do not know. My own observation tells me that the endurance of the human nervous system is limited. By means of the G.P.U. Stalin can trap his victim in an abyss of black despair, humiliation and infamy, until the victim takes upon himself the most monstrous crimes. The Moscow trials do not dishonour the revolution – they are the outcome of reaction. Nor do they dishonour the old generation of Bolsheviks; they only demonstrate that even Bolsheviks are made of flesh and blood, and that they do not resist forever when the pendulum of death swings over their heads. It is time, my listeners, it is high time, to recognize that a new aristocracy has been formed in the Soviet Union. The October revolution proceeded under the banner of equality. The bureaucracy embodies a monstrous inequality. The bureaucracy is afraid of the people. The lava of the revolution is not yet cold. The bureaucracy cannot admit to crushing the discontented and the critical merely because the critics demand a reduction of inequality. Hence they must bear false witness against the opposition. The whole policy of the new aristocracy is a frame-up . . . the frame-up is a system. When the Stalinists call us traitors, there is in that accusation not only hatred, but also a certain sort of sincerity. They think that we betray the interest of that holy cast of bureaucrats, marshals and generals who alone, they think, are capable of 'constructing socialism', but who in fact are discrediting the very idea of socialism. Socialism is impossible without the independent activity of the masses and the flourishing of the human personality. Stalinism tramples on both. An open revolutionary conflict between the people and the new despotism is inevitable. Stalin's regime is doomed. And even if our generation happens to be too weak to establish socialism throughout the world, we will hand the spotless banner down to our children. The struggle far transcends the importance of individuals, of factions or of parties. It is the struggle for the future of all mankind. It will be severe. It will be lengthy. Who ever seeks physical comfort and spiritual calm, let him step aside. But all those for whom the word socialism is not a hollow sound, but the very basis of their moral lives – to those, I say 'Forward!' Threats, persecutions or violence cannot stop us! Be it even over our bleaching bones, the truth will triumph!

After hearings in Mexico, Paris and New York and after thorough investigation of the documents in the case, the Commission of Inquiry passed this verdict: 'On the basis of all the evidence herein stated, we find that the Moscow trials of August 1936 and January 1937 were frame-ups. On the basis of all the evidence herein examined and all the conclusions stated, we find Leon Trotsky and his son Leon Sedov not guilty.' To substantiate this verdict, the Commission of Inquiry published its report in two bulky volumes: *The Case of Leon Trotsky* and *Not Guilty*. At the time, however, the world showed little interest in the Commission's findings. Incredible though this may sound, most people in the West were inclined either to believe in the truth of the Stalinist accusations or at least to assume that these accusations were not quite groundless. Many thought that Stalin's opponents must have formed some sort of fifth column working to overthrow the Soviet regime. The term 'fifth column' had been coined by General Franco or his propagandists during the Spanish civil war, at the time of the siege of Madrid. General Franco boasted that in addition to his four military columns surrounding the capital, a fifth column of his secret supporters was working for him inside Madrid. Stalinist propagandists took over the term and described the Trotskyists, Zinovievists, Bukharinists and other anti-Stalinists as Hitler's fifth column in the U.S.S.R. The trick was clever enough, for who in the democratic West did not wish, on the eve of the Second World War, that Stalin should succeed in crushing Hitler's fifth column, if such a column existed in the Soviet Union? No report of any counter-trial, conducted in remote Mexico, ever reached the Soviet people. We have heard Stalin boasting about the purges at the Eighteenth Party Congress. Here is another important speaker, addressing the same Congress: Nikita Sergeyevich Khrushchev, speaking on 13 March 1939:

Khrushchev: Comrades, you have heard the report about the struggle for communism we have been waging under the leadership of our party, and of its Stalinist Central Committee, under the guidance of our leader of genius, our glorious teacher, our great Stalin. We have gained these successes in a ruthless struggle against the enemies of the working class, against the enemies of the peasantry, against the enemies of our people – in a struggle against the agents of fascist espionage services, the Trotskyists, the Bukharinists and the bourgeois nationalists. Our successes ought not to weaken our will and resolve. Every Bolshevik, every worker, every citizen of our Soviet land is clearly aware that if we have been able to rout all these fascist agents, all these contemptible Trotskyists, Bukharinists and bourgeois nationalists, we are indebted for this primarily to our great leader, our great and glorious Stalin.

Who would have thought that one day the same speaker would denounce Stalin as a villain and tyrant, and would call for an end of the 'cult of Stalin's personality'?

But that day was still far off. In the meantime Stalin was at the pinnacle of power. Even so he felt as if he were sitting on a volcano. The people of the U.S.S.R. were cowed but resentful. The peasantry had not recovered from the shocks of forcible collectivization. The town people had not yet forgotten the years of famine and terror. The armed forces were demoralized by the purge of their commanding officers. And the world was trembling on the brink of the Second World War.

**Right: the Stalin-Hitler Pact —
von Ribbentrop is welcomed to Moscow**

In August 1939, Stalin signed his pact with Hitler, which allowed him to annex the Eastern marches of Poland and to keep the U.S.S.R. out of the world war for twenty-two months, until 21 June 1941. Stalin was now more anxious than ever to rid himself of the menace that he saw in Trotsky, the only survivor of the Bolshevik Old Guard. As long as Trotsky was alive, the Great Purges would not have attained their real object. Trotsky was still untiringly denouncing Stalin, especially the pact with Hitler which Stalin had signed after he had so grotesquely accused Trotsky, Tukhachevsky, Bukharin and the others of collusion with Hitler. At the end of April 1940, Trotsky was addressing this message from Mexico City to the people of the U.S.S.R.

Trotsky: Soviet workers, peasants, soldiers and sailors! You are being deceived. Your newspapers are telling you lies in the interest of Stalin, that super-Cain of our time – and in the interest of his depraved commissars, secretaries and G.P.U. men. Your bureaucracy is blood-thirsty and ruthless at home, but cowardly towards the imperialist powers. This is now the main source of danger to the Soviet Union. Workers and soldiers, you must never surrender to the world bourgeoisie the nationalized industry and the collectivized economy of the U.S.S.R. On this foundation you may still build a new and happier society. But you will do this only if you can overthrow the tyranny of Stalin.

Stalin was more than ever impatient to stifle this voice. On 24 May 1940, in the dead of night, a gang of armed Mexican Stalinists carried out an attempt on Trotsky's life. They subjected Trotsky's bedroom to a hail of bullets, and left convinced that Trotsky and his wife were dead. But the attempt was a failure. Trotsky and his wife had had a narrow escape. The G.P.U. did not give up. The next attempt was to be carried out by a G.P.U. agent who had unobtrusively worked his way into Trotsky's home. Throughout the years of his exile, the G.P.U. had managed to keep an informer either among the members of Trotsky's household or among his close followers. The last of these *agents provocateurs* was a man whose identity has not been officially established even now, although it is almost certain that his name was

Trotsky's assassination —
Mexican police display the murder weapon.
Opposite page:
the assassin, Ramon Mercader

The guard of honour at Trotsky's coffin

Ramon Mercador, and that he was a Spanish Stalinist. He presented himself to Trotsky under the name of 'Fran Jacson', pretending at first to be quite uninterested in politics and then to be converted to Trotsky's views. On 20 August 1940 he came to Trotsky saying that he wished to submit to him an article he had written. In this way he managed to remain alone with Trotsky in the latter's study, and to carry out the attempt. Trotsky had just managed to run through the first page of 'Jacson's' manuscript when a terrific blow came down upon his head. This is how the assassin himself later described the scene: 'I had put down my raincoat on a piece of furniture. I grasped the ice axe (which I had hidden in the coat) and, closing my eyes, I brought it down on Trotsky's head with all my strength. I thought that after this mighty blow he would be dead at once, but he uttered a terrible piercing cry – I shall hear that cry all my life.' His skull smashed, his face covered with blood, Trotsky jumped up, hurled at the murderer whatever object was at hand, books, ink-pots, even a dictaphone, and then grappled with him. It had all taken only three or four minutes. The 'terrible piercing cry' had brought Trotsky's wife and secretaries to their feet, but it took a few moments for them to realize whence it had come and to rush in its direction. During those moments a furious struggle was going on in the study: Trotsky's last struggle. He fought like a tiger, wrestling with the murderer, biting his hand and wresting the ice axe from him. The murderer was so astonished that he did not strike another blow. Then Trotsky, no longer able to stand up, straining all his will not to collapse at his enemy's feet, slowly staggered back.

Thus the death sentence was carried out on the man who *in absentia* had been the chief defendant in all the Moscow trials. On his desk, bespattered with blood from the skull-wound, lay the manuscript of his last book, a book on Stalin. It contained these words:

Trotsky: Nero too was, like Stalin, the product of his age. Yet when he perished his statues were smashed and his name was everywhere effaced. The vengeance of history is more terrible than the vengeance of the most powerful General Secretary. I venture to think this is consoling.

A walk in the Kremlin, 1948: left to right, Stalin, Beria (Yezhov's successor), Mikoyan arm-in-arm with Malenkov

Historians may dispute what might have happened to Stalin if he had not carried out the Great Purges. Would he have remained in power to the end? Or would his critics and enemies have overthrown him? The fact is that by means of the Great Purges Stalin destroyed, for a long time to come, any possibility of an alternative government in the Soviet Union. And so, unchallenged and unchallengeable, he dominated the Soviet scene throughout the years of the Second World War, while the Soviet Union endured the Nazi invasion, and while its armies sustained heavy defeats. Then, when the thunderous Soviet victories and conquests arrived, Stalin's figure assumed, in the eyes of the world, the stature of a colossus: he overshadowed the whole scene of world politics. To Eastern Europe, his armies carried revolution on the points of their bayonets. By 1949 Stalinist regimes had been established in Poland, Czechoslovakia, Hungary, East Germany, Rumania, Bulgaria and Albania.

With the Stalinist regime there came to these countries the Great Purges also. The year 1949 brought the trials of Slansky and Clementis in Prague, of Laszlo Rajk and comrades in Budapest, and of Trajcho Kostov and his group in Sofia. In Warsaw, Gomulka was imprisoned. This was in the middle of the feud between Stalin and Tito; Slansky, Clementis, Rajk, Kostov and Gomulka were all accused of conspiring with Tito, of being Trotskyists and Bukharinists, and of being American, British, French, German and other spies. It was a peculiar feature of those post-war trials that their victims were also denounced as Zionists, and that these trials (and the propaganda that surrounded them) were conducted in tones of strident anti-Semitism.

About the same time, after an interval of nearly ten years, Stalin staged a new series of purges in the Soviet Union. In 1950 Nikolay Voznesensky, a member of the Politbureau and head of the State Planning Commission, the man who had directed the Soviet economy throughout the Second World War, was executed in the course of a purge connected with the so-called Leningrad affair. Another victim of that purge was Rodionov, Prime Minister of the Russian Federal Republic. Then there was the purge of Jewish writers and artists; then the Georgian purge; and finally the affair of the so-called 'doctors' plot', which was announced shortly before Stalin's death. The scope and the intentions of all these purges are still not fully explained. The Kremlin doctors, many of them Jews, were accused of attempts to poison Stalin and the Marshals of the Soviet Armed Forces, and of working on the instructions of an American Jewish organization.

It all looked as if, just before his death, Stalin had been preparing a repetition of the gigantic trials of 1936–8: a new Witches' Sabbath, with mass accusations, mass confessions and mass executions. On 5 March 1953, however, Stalin died. While he was still on his deathbed, the members of the Praesidium stopped all preparations for the new purges. The Kremlin doctors were at once freed from prison, and rehabilitated. All charges against them were declared null and void. This is what Khrushchev said about the case, three years after Stalin's death:

Khrushchev: And now, comrades, a few words about the affair of the Kremlin doctors. (ANIMATION IN THE AUDIENCE.) Actually there was no such affair. All that there was was a declaration by the woman Timashuk, a doctor, who, probably on the instigation of our security organs, wrote a letter to Stalin in which she said that the Kremlin doctors were applying improper methods of medical treatment. This was enough for Stalin to jump to the conclusion that the doctors were engaged in a plot. He issued orders to arrest a whole group of our most eminent medical specialists. He personally supervised the investigation and prescribed the method of interrogation. He ordered Academician Vinogradov to be put in chains and another doctor to be beaten. To comrade Ignatiev, our former Minister of State Security, Stalin said curtly: 'If you do not obtain confessions from the

Above left: Vlado Clementis arm-in-arm with Vyshinsky. Above right: Laszlo Rajk (second from right) under interrogation. Opposite page: three of the accused in the 'Doctors' Plot'. Top to bottom, Feldman, Vovsi and Kogan

Stalin lying in state in the Hall of Columns, the House of Trade Unions, Moscow, March 6th 1953

Above: at Stalin's bier, left to right,
Khrushchev, Beria, Malenkov,
Bulganin, Voroshilov and Kaganovich.
Below: the funeral procession

doctors, we shall shorten you by a head.' (UPROAR IN THE AUDIENCE.) Stalin personally called the examining magistrate and told him how he was to examine the doctors. The method was very simple indeed: 'Beat them, beat them, and then beat them again!' We felt that the arrested doctors might well be innocent. We had known some of them personally; we had been their patients. But the case was so presented that no one could verify the circumstances. When, after Stalin's death, we looked at the case, we found it to have been fabricated from beginning to end.

The arrested doctors could not have figured as the chief defendants in any purge-trial Stalin may have planned. They could be presented only as the tools of other people, people far more influential and ambitious politically. Who were those people?

Khrushchev: Evidently, Stalin had planned to finish off the old members of the Politbureau. He often said that the old Politbureau members should be replaced . . . We can assume that he had a scheme for their annihilation – he was out to destroy those who could bear witness to his crimes . . . He had already reduced the Politbureau to impotence; its members no longer had any say in important state affairs. One of our oldest members, Marshall Voroshilov, was for several years denied access to the conferences of the Political Bureau. Stalin forbade him . . . to receive any Politbureau documents. Whenever a Politbureau session was to be held, comrade Voroshilov telephoned to ask whether he would at least be allowed to attend. Stalin laboured under the absurd and ridiculous suspicion that comrade Voroshilov was an English agent. (LAUGHTER IN THE AUDIENCE.) Yes, an English agent. A special tapping device was installed in comrade Voroshilov's home. (INDIGNATION IN THE AUDIENCE.) In this way, Stalin eliminated yet another Politbureau member – comrade Andrey Andreyev. And at the session of the Central Committee held just after the Nineteenth Congress, before the end of 1952, Stalin spoke against Vyacheslav Mikhailovich Molotov and Anastas Ivanovich Mikoyan, hinting that these old party leaders were guilty of some ill-defined crime. If Stalin had remained

at the helm for another few months, Comrades Molotov and Mikoyan might not have been with us today. (TUMULT IN THE HALL.)

Despite his own zeal for Stalinism, Khrushchev himself has told how Stalin liked to humiliate his future successor in front of other Politbureau members and strangers, ordering him to perform the gopak, a dance not perhaps quite suitable for performance by a middle-aged statesman.

Khrushchev: Yes, comrades, Stalin was a very distrustful man, diseased with suspicion. We knew this from our work with him. He would look at a man and say: 'Why are your eyes so shifty today? Why are you turning away so much today? Why are you unable to look me in the eyes?' Everywhere, and in everyone, Stalin saw an enemy or a spy. Wielding unlimited power, he indulged in great wilfulness. He choked you morally and physically. In those days I often talked with Nikolay Alexandrovich Bulganin. Once we were travelling alone together in a car and Bulganin said to me: 'Sometimes one goes to Stalin at Stalin's invitation, as a friend; and as one sits there with him one does not quite know where one is going to be sent next: home or to gaol?'

And so at Stalin's death the men of his entourage breathed with relief, and decided to do away with the terroristic purges, to proclaim an amnesty for political prisoners, to curtail the powers of the G.P.U. and to carry out a number of reforms in the governmental system. To the people of the Soviet Union, these reforms were most welcome. To justify the reforms Khrushchev and his colleagues had to dispel the Stalin myth. They had to smash the idol to whom they had bowed for so long. Khrushchev's role was especially awkward. While at the Twentieth Congress in February 1956 he was denouncing the late dictator, many people could still

Below: Three minutes' silence is observed for Stalin throughout the Soviet Union on March 9th, 1953

Mr and Mrs Vyshinsky (left) with Mr and Mrs Molotov at a reception in the Kremlin in 1947. Polina Molotov was a victim of Stalin's anti-semitism; deported to Kazakistan in 1951, she was only freed after his death

recall the eulogies of Stalin that he had pronounced during Stalin's lifetime. Hence the embarrassed contradictions and inconsistencies in which Khrushchev involved himself.

Khrushschev: Comrades, Stalin's acts were not the outcome of persuasion, or of patient co-operation with people. He imposed his ideas. He demanded absolute submission. Whoever was critical of any concept of Stalin's . . . was doomed to moral and physical annihilation.

Thus Khrushchev the de-Stalinizer. But as he spoke, an echo of his old voice seemed still to reverberate:

Khrushchev: Comrades, we have been pursuing our struggle under the guidance of a leader of genius, of our great teacher, our glorious Stalin. We have been pursuing this struggle against all the agents of foreign fascist espionage networks – against the Trotskyists, Bukharinists, bourgeois nationalists and all the other enemies of the people. Glory to our great Stalin.

And here again is Khrushchev the de-Stalinizer:

Khrushchev: It was Stalin who originated the concept 'enemy of the people'. In a controversy, this term automatically rendered it unnecessary to prove anyone's errors. This term – 'enemy of the people' – was used to justify the most cruel repression, the violation of all normal revolutionary legality, the destruction of anyone who dissented from Stalin in any degree whatsoever, of anyone who was suspected merely of hostile intent, of anyone who merely had a bad reputation. Many absolutely innocent people, who had rendered great services to our party, were victimized in this way.

In the same breath, however, he stated:
Khrushchev: The party had fought a serious fight against the Trotskyites, Bukharinites and other deviationists – and it disarmed them all ideologically, as enemies of Leninism. As a result of

Left: Nikita Khrushchev. Overleaf: Marshals Rokossovksy and Voroshilov

that fight the party gained in strength, and Stalin played a positive role in this. It was a stubborn and difficult fight, but a necessary one: the policies of the Trotskyites, Zinovievites and Bukharinites would have led towards the restoration of capitalism.

Thus, in nearly all his speeches, we can hear the duet, as it were, between the two Khrushchevs: Khrushchev the de-Stalinizer and Khrushchev the Stalinist. He has been smashing his idol with one hand and trying to put it together again with the other. It is the fact that the people of the Soviet Union had grown sick of Stalinism that had again and again forced Moscow's ruling group, and Khrushchev personally, to go ahead with de-Stalinization, and to go even beyond the limit at which they would have preferred to stop. Hence the strange explosive tempo of de-Stalinization, the suddenness of its crucial acts and the great emotional turbulence that surrounds it. At the Twentieth and the Twenty-Second Party Congresses, survivors of the Stalinist purges were present, demanding justice for themselves and for their comrades and that the whole truth about the purges be told. The same demands were made by the children, brothers and friends of many dead victims. And the Soviet people of the 1950s and the 1960s were very different from the people of the 1930s, when they helplessly endured the purges and accepted Stalin's falsifications. The people of today are far better educated and far more self-confident. Not only would they not submit to anything like the Stalinist terror, but their sense of dignity is outraged by what has happened in the past – about which they want to know the truth, and the whole truth. It was in response to such moods and such demands that Khrushchev declared:

Khrushchev: Stalin's arbitrary behaviour encouraged arbitrariness in others. Mass arrests and deportations, and executions without trials, created conditions of insecurity, fear and despair. What a difference there was, comrades, between the actions of Lenin and of Stalin! Lenin used severe methods only when this was absolutely necessary, when the exploiting classes were still vigorously opposing the revolution, and when the struggle assumed the sharpest form, the form of civil war. Stalin used mass reprisals when the revolution was already victorious, when the Soviet state was strong and consolidated. Again and again he showed his intolerance and brutality, and abused his power. This was especially true during the last fifteen years of his life. He hardly ever called a session of the Central Committee. In all the years of the Second World War, not a single plenary session of the Committee was held.

Returning to the Great Purges and to Stalin's role in them, Khrushchev speaks of the price Russia paid for Stalin's autocracy, especially in the Second World War. Stalin ignored all warnings about Hitler's preparations for the attack on Russia, including a warning from Winston Churchill. And the Red Army found itself engaged in battle after its officers' corps had been half destroyed in the purges.

Khrushchev: Very grievous consequences followed the annihilation by Stalin of our military commanders, for, comrades, in our armed forces the purge started literally from the level of company and battalion commander, and reached to the highest staff officers. Those commanders who had gained battle experience in the Spanish civil war were liquidated almost to a man. For several years, officers of all ranks (and even privates) were taught to 'unmask' their superiors as hidden enemies. This could not fail to undermine morale and discipline. Comrades, among the commanders who have managed to survive, despite severe torture endured in prison, among these are such excellent generals as Marshal Rokossovsky, Generals Gorbatov, Meretskov and others, some of whom are present here. But many of our best commanders perished in the concentration camps and gaols. Hence the danger to which our fatherland was exposed in the first period of the war.

Remember that in the last war the Soviet Union lost about twenty million men in dead alone. Every family lost a father, a brother or a son. What Khrushchev was telling all these bereaved families was that if the Great Purges had not crippled the Red Army, they might not have suffered all those terrible losses.

Khrushchev: And during the war, comrades, we also saw whole peoples deported, upon Stalin's orders, from their native lands. Thus at the end of December 1943 the whole population of the Autonomous Kalmyk Republic was deported. In March 1944 all the Chechen and Ingush peoples were driven from their lands. In April all Tartars were sent away to faraway places. The Ukrainians were not deported only because there were too many of them, and there was no place to deport them. After the war, Stalin became even more capricious, irritable and brutal. His persecution mania reached unbelievable dimensions. Yet, comrades, he was convinced that all he was doing was in the interest of the working class, whom he must defend against the plots of our enemies and against attacks from the imperialist camp . . . He considered that what he was doing ought to be done in the interest of the party, of the toiling

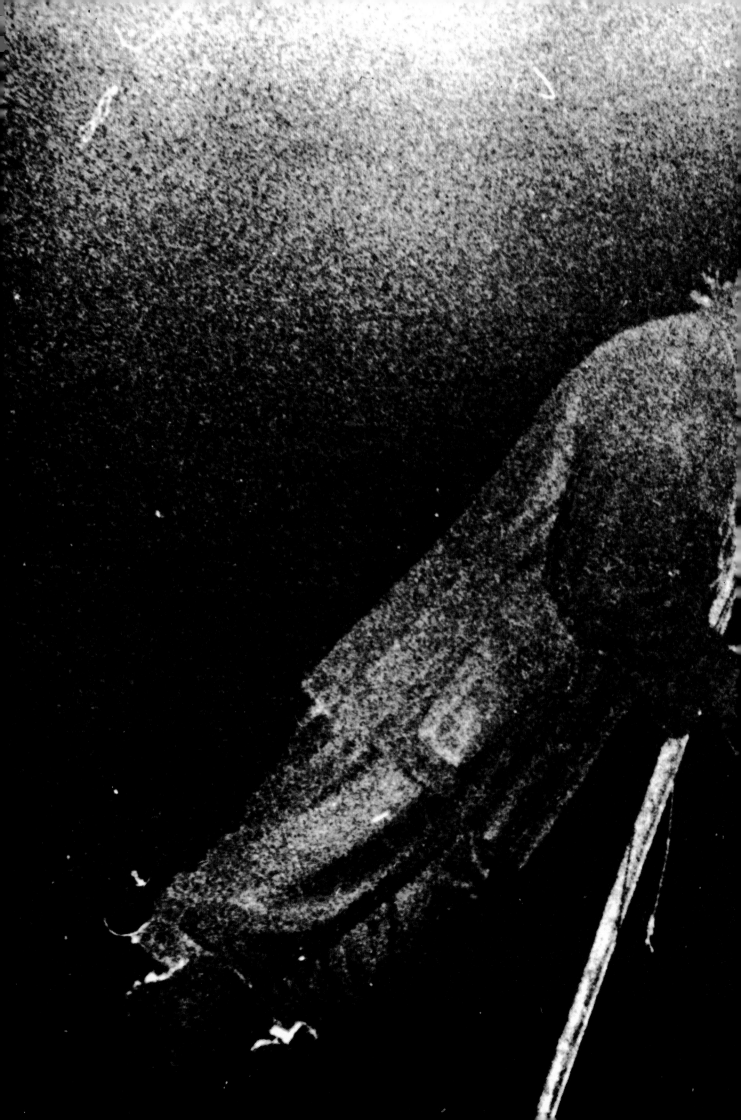

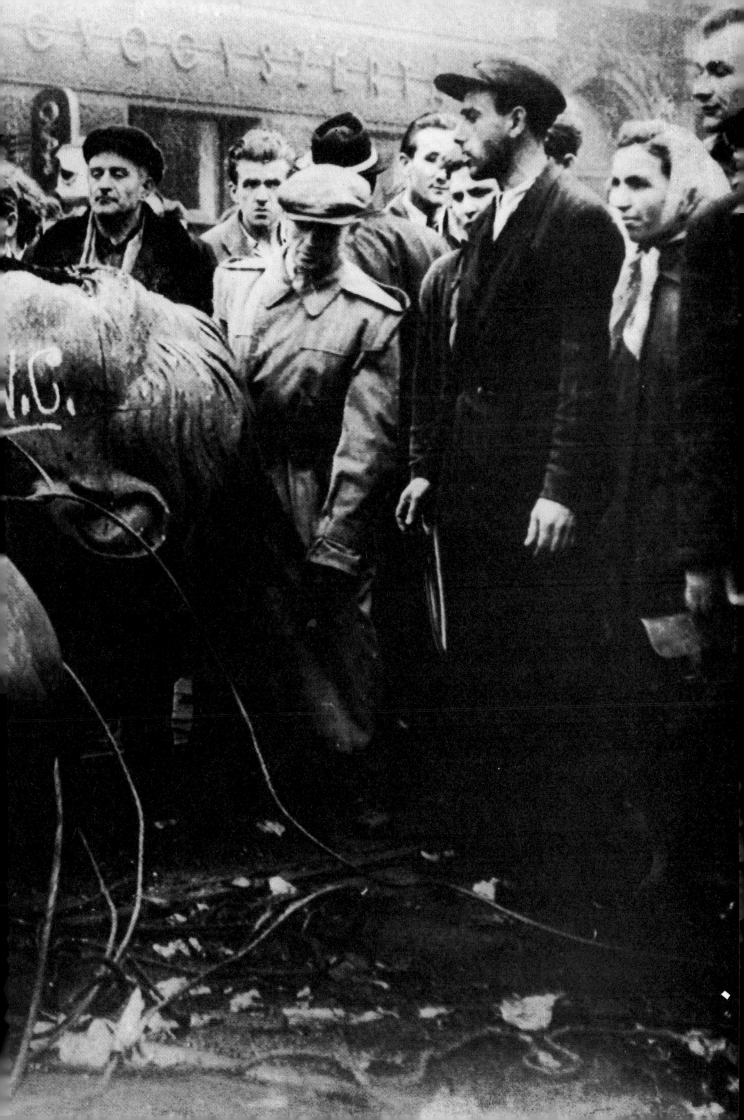

masses – in the interest of the revolution, and of socialism and communism. In this lay the whole tragedy.

This is what Khrushchev was saying in 1956. It took another five years before the Twenty-Second Congress of the Soviet Communist Party decided that the embalmed body of Stalin should be evicted from the Mausoleum in Red Square. As Trotsky had predicted, Stalin's statues were destroyed as Nero's were, and his name was everywhere defaced: even Stalingrad was renamed Volvograd.

Yet, even now, the full truth about the Great Purges has not yet been revealed in the U.S.S.R. The old accusations against Stalin's opponents, against Trotsky, Zinoviev, Kamenev, Bukharin, Radek and the others, the accusations of conspiracy, treason and espionage, are no longer repeated. Nor, however, have most of these victims of the purges been clearly rehabilitated. Only to some of them has justice been done posthumously. Thus Marshal Tukhachevsky and the generals who perished with him have been fully rehabilitated. Yet neither the records of their trial, if there ever was such a trial, nor the records of the investigation that led to rehabilitation, have ever been made public. Every now and then the world learns from a casual article or note in a Soviet newspaper about another important act of rehabilitation. One day, for instance, it is the rehabilitation of Antonov-Ovseenko, another day that of Krestinsky, both eminent leaders of the Trotskyist opposition in the 1920s.

Remember that virtually the whole case against Rykov, Bukharin, Rakovsky, Yagoda and the others had been based on Krestinsky's confessions. It was Krestinsky who maintained that he had repeatedly and clandestinely met Trotsky outside Russia, had conspired with him, had conferred with him in the presence of German generals, and had transferred millions of Goldmarks and dollars from the German General Staff to Trotsky and his son. It was Krestinsky who had depicted Trotsky and his friends as agents of Hitler, of the Mikado, of the British Military Intelligence; who had accused them of organizing attempts on the lives of Stalin, Molotov and Kaganovich; of having caused railway catastrophes, colliery explosions and mass poisoning of workers. Now we are told that the man who made all these confessions was absolutely innocent! Yet those whom his confessions implicated are still denied an open and unequivocal rehabilitation. Khrushchev and his colleagues still hesitate. Are they disturbed by echoes from the past?

Khrushchev: Comrades, we have been pursuing our struggle against these enemies of the people under the guidance of a leader of genius, our great and glorious Stalin.

Above: Stalin's body is evicted
from Lenin's mausoleum, October 1961
Opposite page: Budapest, 1956 —
Stalin's boots alone remain

Andrei Vyshinsky, who became Soviet Ambassador to the United Nations, died of a heart attack in New York in 1954